What they don't t...

INVADERS

> DON'T PICK YOUR NOSE!

> PICK THIS BOOK!

By Bob Fowke

Dedicated to the God Jupiter – in case he exists.

A division of Hodder Headline Limited

> Pay attention, reader! And don't keep me waiting - I know how to deal with barbarians like you! My name's Ruflus Disciplin - I'm an officer in the Roman army. Fall in line there and I'll show how we Romans conquered Britain and tamed the British barbarians.

This edition of *What They Don't Tell You About Romans in Britain*, *What They Don't Tell You About Anglo-Saxons* and *What They Don't Tell You About Vikings* first published by Hodder Children's Books 2001.

Cover: Viking Invader. Picture supplied by Hodder Wayland Picture Library.

What They Don't Tell You About Romans in Britain first published as a single volume in Great Britain in 1998 by Hodder Children's Books.

Text and illustrations copyright © Bob Fowke 1998

The right of Bob Fowke to be identified as the author of the Work has been asserted by him in accordance with the Copyright, Designs and Patents Act 1988.

10 9 8 7 6 5 4 3 2 1

All rights reserved. No part of this publication may be reproduced, stored in a retrieval system, or transmitted, in any form or by any means, without the prior written permission of the publisher, nor be otherwise circulated in any form of binding or cover other than that in which it is published and without a similar condition being imposed on the subsequent purchaser.

ISBN 0 340 84380 2

A Catalogue record for this book is available from the British Library.

Printed by The Guernsey Press Ltd, Guernsey, Channel Islands.

Hodder Children's Books
A division of Hodder Headline Limited
338 Euston Road
London NW1 3BH

CONTENTS

BEFORE WE BEGIN
ONE SPRING MORNING — Page 5

ROME ON THE ROAM
THE EMPIRE MADE EASY — Page 6

BARMY BRITONS
BRITAIN BEFORE THE ROMANS — Page 12

BOOT CAMPS
- OR SHOULD WE SAY SANDAL CAMPS?
THE ROMAN ARMY — Page 24

THEY CAME, THEY SAW, THEY TOOK
ROADS, WALLS AND THINGS IN BETWEEN — Page 35

SLAVES AND LADDERS
THE SOCIAL LADDER, FROM SLAVES TO EMPERORS WITH RUNGS IN BETWEEN — Page 45

NITTY GRITTY CITIES
FANCY FORUMS AND BUSY BASILICAS — Page 61

Watch out for the *Sign of the Foot*! Whenever you see this sign in the book it means there are some more details at the *FOOT* of the page. Like here.

Drusilla's villa
Life in the country
Page 69

The good life
Living it up at banquets, and other bashes
Page 77

Gladiators!
Leisure time the Roman way
Page 89

Odd gods
Glorious gods and critical Christians
Page 105

Beastly barbarians
The beginning of the end
Page 113

Finis
Dark ages pages
Page 119

Index	Page 123
Now read on	Page 126
About the author	Page 127

BEFORE WE BEGIN

ONE SPRING MORNING

Two men with spiky blond hair are sitting on the white cliffs of Dover. If you walk up behind them slowly, you might mistake their heads for two hedgehogs which have settled down to look at the view. The two men are **Ancient Britons**. They gaze out to sea.

It's a fine spring morning. The waves sparkle beneath them. Behind them, the country is green, rich and fertile. AD 43 is a great time to be alive - or at least it should be ...

Ancient Briton is a term usually used to describe someone who lived in Britain in prehistoric times, that is, when people didn't yet read and write.

ROME ON THE ROAM

THE EMPIRE MADE EASY

Unfortunately for the Ancient Britons, in AD 43 the mighty Emperor Tiberius Claudius Drusus Nero Germanicus (10 BC - AD 54), or Claudius for short, had ordered a vast army of Roman soldiers to invade Britain.

HI CLAUDIUS!

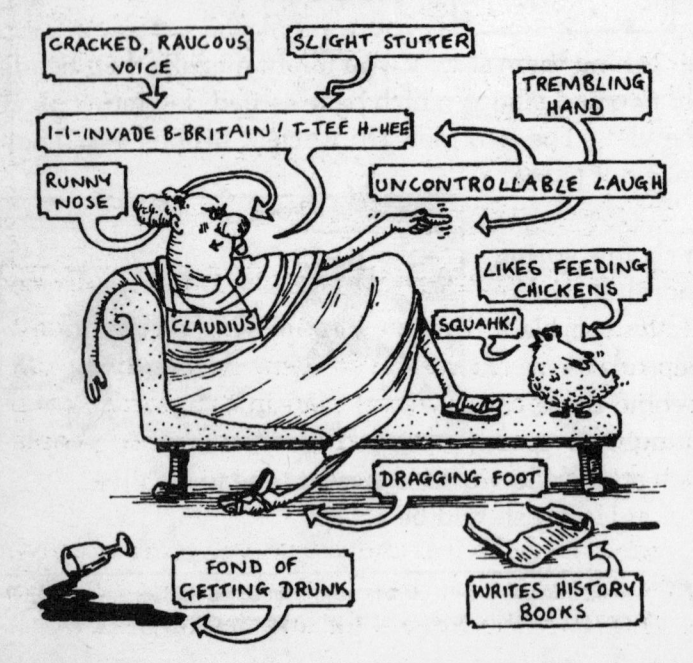

- CRACKED, RAUCOUS VOICE
- SLIGHT STUTTER
- I-I-INVADE B-BRITAIN! T-TEE H-HEE
- TREMBLING HAND
- RUNNY NOSE
- UNCONTROLLABLE LAUGH
- LIKES FEEDING CHICKENS
- CLAUDIUS
- SQUAWK!
- DRAGGING FOOT
- FOND OF GETTING DRUNK
- WRITES HISTORY BOOKS

WHY CLAUDIUS?

Claudius became Emperor of Rome after the murder of his mad nephew, the Emperor Caligula, just after one o'clock on 24th January AD 41. Caligula's killers, their swords still bloody, saw Claudius' slippers sticking out from beneath a curtain where he was hiding. They decided to make him Emperor because they couldn't find anybody else suitable - Claudius would do because he was a member of the Roman ruling family.

THOUGHT YOU'D SLIP AWAY DID YOU?

At that time the Roman Empire was the mightiest empire the world has ever seen, so Claudius had become the most powerful man in the world - even though he was a drunkard, whom most people thought was weak in the head!

Claudius needed a war and a victory in order to prove to the Roman people what a good emperor he could be. That's why he ordered the invasion of Britain.

7

THE ROMAN EMPIRE IN AD 43

The Romans were ruthlessly efficient and they were brilliant soldiers. They built an army which was the best in the world for more than a thousand years. And with that army they conquered an empire which lasted in the west until AD 476. (In the east the *Byzantine* Empire or Eastern Roman Empire continued until AD 1453 when it was finally overrun by the Turks.)

BARBARIANS

BARBARIANS

BRITAIN (SOON TO BE CONQUERED). THE ROMANS RULED BRITAIN FOR NEARLY 400 YEARS, A FIFTH OF BRITISH HISTORY FROM THAT TIME TO THIS.

ROME (POPULATION AROUND TWO MILLION, FOUNDED IN 753 BC)

ROMAN-RULED AFRICA

SEARCHING FOR CLUES

The Roman Empire soared like a comet for hundreds of years and then fell like a stone. Britain was part of that Empire and part of the fall. Since it all happened an incredibly long time ago, you might expect that

---

This is about the same as the population of modern Birmingham.

nothing much would be left to tell us what went on. Well, a lot has disappeared, but the Empire was so big and it went on for such a long time that there are still plenty of clues as to what the Ancient Romans were like and how they lived:

🔑 Many of their books have survived in old libraries. We know the names of their famous writers, some of whom wrote about the British

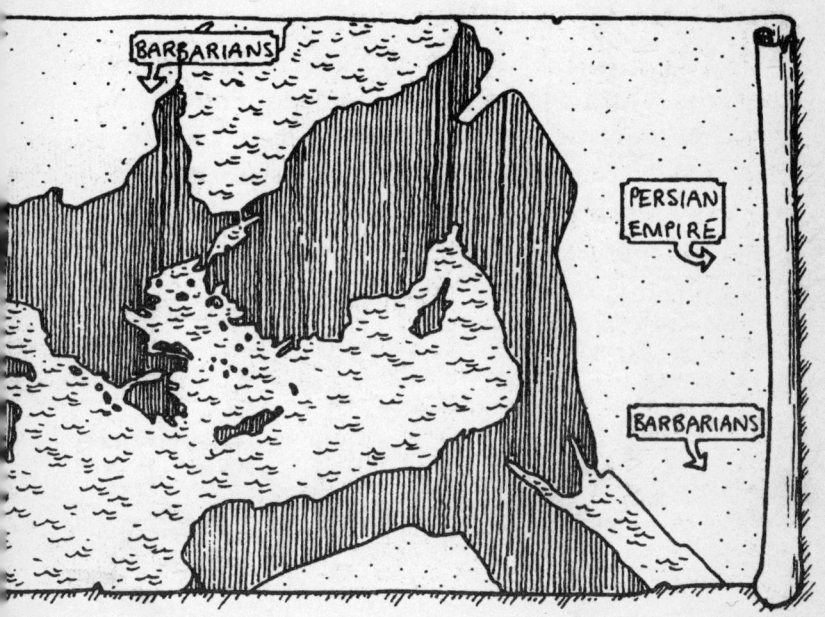

[map showing BARBARIANS, PERSIAN EMPIRE, BARBARIANS]

and their battles with the Romans, and we can read about Roman generals and emperors.

🔑 They built to last. The countries they once ruled are littered with the vast remains of theatres, temples, aqueducts 🦶 and even whole cities.

🦶 *Aqueducts* are artificial channels which carry water above the ground, sometimes for long distances.

- There are over a million Roman inscriptions which can still be read on old gravestones and monuments.

- Archaeologists dig up the remains of everyday objects, such as old pots or hair combs. These help us to understand how the Romans used to live.

THAT'S ALL OF US AULUS

Following Claudius' orders, in AD 43 Aulus Plautius, the Roman commander in Gaul (modern France), had gathered an army of forty thousand men, plus some elephants to impress the natives, at Gesoriacum (the modern French port of Boulogne). He was to invade Britain as soon as possible.

This would not be the first Roman invasion of Britain. In 55-56 BC, nearly a hundred years before, the Britons had been beaten by the famous Roman general Julius Caesar. But Caesar had to return to Rome for political reasons before his conquest of Britain was complete.

Archaeologists are historians who look for clues about the past by searching for buried remains.

After Caesar's troops had left, the Britons had gone back to their 'savage' Celtic ways, as the Romans saw them. In fact by AD 43 the Britons were helping rebellious Gauls to fight the Romans, egged on by *Druids* who were based in Britain. Plautius and his Emperor Claudius knew that they had to beat the Britons if there was to be peace in Gaul.

In other words, they were going to teach those pesky Britons a lesson. No wonder the two Ancient Britons were sitting on the white cliffs of Dover; they were looking for the sails of the Roman invasion fleet.

They wouldn't have long to wait.

Druids were the priests of the Ancient Britons and Gauls. More on them later.

BARMY BRITONS

BRITAIN BEFORE THE ROMANS

MUD IN BRITAIN

In AD 43, Britain was divided into a crazy patchwork of tribal kingdoms ruled by small-time royalty. The aristocracy tended to live in hill-forts with high earth walls, probably topped with wooden fences. You can still see the remains of these hill-forts on the tops of many hills today.

WHICH TRIBE DO YOU BELONG TO?
If you had been alive in AD 43, which tribe would have ruled over the region where you live today?

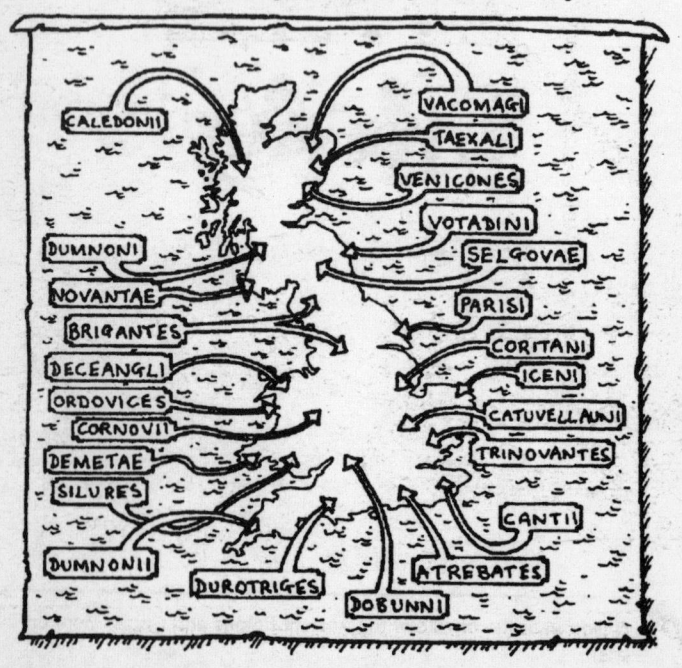

CALEDONII
VACOMAGI
TAEXALI
VENICONES
VOTADINI
DUMNONI
SELGOVAE
NOVANTAE
PARISI
BRIGANTES
DECEANGLI
CORITANI
ORDOVICES
ICENI
CORNOVII
CATUVELLAUNI
DEMETAE
TRINOVANTES
SILURES
CANTII
DUMNONII
DUROTRIGES
ATREBATES
DOBUNNI

Whether inside the walls of the hill-forts or out in the country, people lived in circular huts made of mud daubed over sticks and twigs 👣. The country was wild and wooded. There were massive areas of thick forest where bears and wolves roamed freely. Between the forests the people were mostly farmers who worked small fields around their farms.

Actually the Ancient Britons weren't total savages, they did produce some goods to sell. Merchants from the civilizations of the Mediterranean had been sailing to south-west England since the time of the Ancient Greeks, at least four hundred years before, to barter for tin, leather, slaves and other goods.

👣 This mixture of mud and sticks is called *wattle and daub*.

These goods were exchanged for luxury items, such as wine and decorated bowls. The Ancient Britons were very fond of wine and valued it highly. Aristocrats would sometimes exchange a healthy slave for a single *amphora* 👣.

DINNER DANGERS!

The Ancient Britons were *Celts*, as were many of the people of northern Europe. Early Celts spoke *Celtic* and liked head hunting and human sacrifice. (The doors of the early Celts were hung with the heads of their enemies). Even in Roman times they would sacrifice a child before any major battle in order to foresee the future. The child would be cut open and any unusual features of the *entrails*, or insides, would be regarded as clues to understanding the future. The Romans did the same sort of thing but only with animals.

> HMM. THE LIVER'S HEALTHY. PERHAPS WE'LL <u>LIVE</u> TO FIGHT ANOTHER DAY!

👣 An *amphora* was a large earthenware jar used for storing and carrying liquids and other goods.

Above all, the Celts loved fighting and fought each other at the slightest opportunity. At their feasts the thigh bone was always given to the bravest hero. Warriors would sometimes fight to the death over drumsticks!

Celts were described by the Romans as being large and fierce with blond hair. They probably looked much like the majority of people of modern England - although you might not want to ask one to dinner!

I'LL HAVE THE DRUMSTICK!

OF COURSE - ANYTHING YOU SAY!

The modern Irish and Welsh describe themselves as Celtic, but they look a lot different to the Celts who lived in England when the Romans invaded. In fact early Irish aristocrats often dyed their hair blond to fit the fashionable Celtic image of that time.

COMPARE THE HAIR

CELTIC WARRIOR

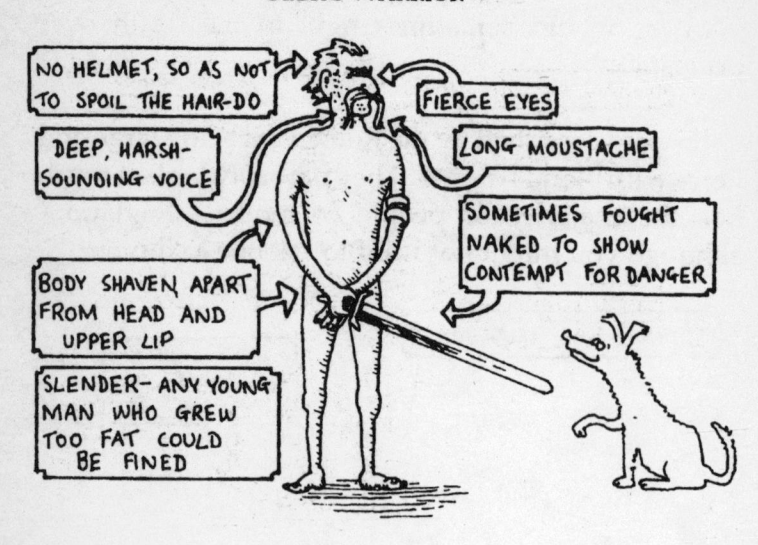

- NO HELMET, SO AS NOT TO SPOIL THE HAIR-DO
- FIERCE EYES
- DEEP, HARSH-SOUNDING VOICE
- LONG MOUSTACHE
- SOMETIMES FOUGHT NAKED TO SHOW CONTEMPT FOR DANGER
- BODY SHAVEN, APART FROM HEAD AND UPPER LIP
- SLENDER — ANY YOUNG MAN WHO GREW TOO FAT COULD BE FINED

CELTIC LADY

- EYEBROWS DYED BLACK WITH BERRY JUICE
- LONG FAIR HAIR — DYED IF NECESSARY — DESCRIBED BY ONE ROMAN WRITER AS A 'STREAMING MANE'
- CHEEKS REDDENED WITH A HERB CALLED RUAM
- HARSH VOICE
- STRONG WHITE ARMS. THE WOMEN WERE DESCRIBED BY SICULUS, A ROMAN WRITER, AS STRONGER THAN THE MEN, AND FOND OF QUARRELLING

Roman writers tended to exaggerate about the Celts.

Roman Gentleman

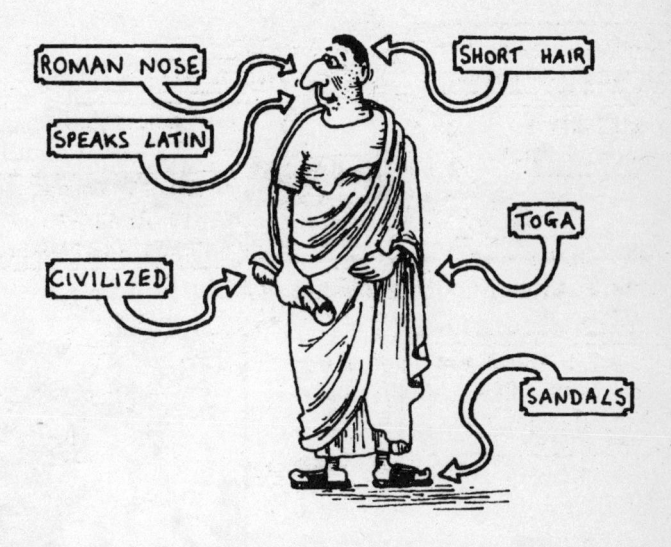

- ROMAN NOSE
- SPEAKS LATIN
- CIVILIZED
- SHORT HAIR
- TOGA
- SANDALS

Roman Lady

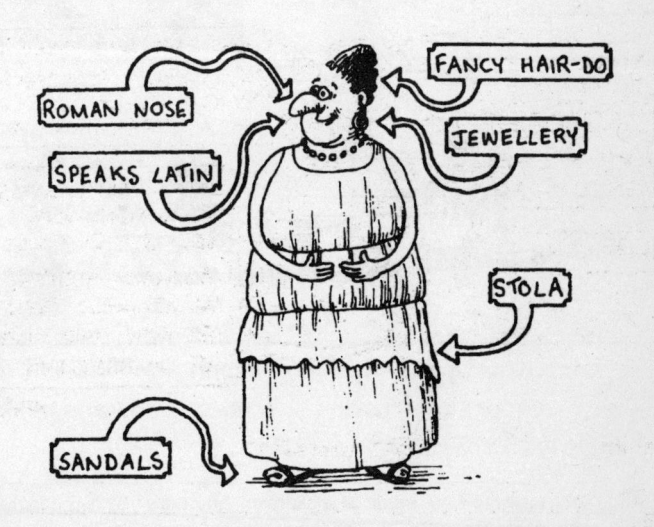

- ROMAN NOSE
- SPEAKS LATIN
- FANCY HAIR-DO
- JEWELLERY
- STOLA
- SANDALS

CLAUDIUS MAKES HIS MOVE

AD 43, Aulus Plautius sets sail from Boulogne with an army of 40,000 men.

They land on the south coast of England and fight a two-day battle against the defending Celts. The Celtic chariots 👣 are no match for the disciplined Roman legions.

The Roman army marches north and the British tribes give way before them, taking their belongings and herds of animals with them.

👣 War chariots were made of wickerwork and drawn by two ponies. The charioteer drove the chariot to the thick of the battle, then the warrior jumped out and fought on foot.

The Romans capture Camulodunum (modern Colchester), the largest British town at that time. Caratacus and Togodumnus, the wild sons of the powerful British king Cunobelin - now dead - govern Camulodunum. These two young men are the leaders of British resistance to Rome. Togodumnus will not live much longer.

Claudius enters Camulodunum in triumph, while Roman armies fan out across the land.

Caratacus the young British leader flees to take up the fight elsewhere.

A TALE OF TWO Cs

Caratacus

The British leader Caratacus escaped into Wales. He kept on fighting bravely until the Romans defeated him and took his wife and children prisoner. Then Caratacus took refuge in the kingdom of the Brigantes in the north of England which was still free of Roman rule. The Brigantes were a primitive tribe of nomads who tended large herds of cattle. They bred the best chariot ponies in Britain and they hated the Romans as much as anybody.

Cartimandua

Cartimandua was queen of the Brigantes. Unlike many of her people, she was friendly towards the Romans, or at least she didn't want to offend them by giving refuge to their main enemy, Caratacus.

In AD 51 Cartimandua handed Caratacus over to the Roman governor of Britain. Caratacus was taken in chains to Rome.

Her name meant 'Sleek Filly'

TRIUMPH!

When he ordered the invasion of Britain, Claudius didn't just want to teach the Britons a lesson. He was after a really big *triumph* to impress the people back in Rome. A triumph wasn't just a victory in the sense of the word today. It was a glittering parade through the streets of Rome and it was only granted to the victors of specially important battles. Claudius needed a major triumph to prove that he was a hero, not just a middle-aged man with a stammer who had been found hiding behind a curtain.

IMPERIAL MATERIAL

CALIGULA IST EIN SCHWEINHUND!

SCHNURGFITZ!

JA! GURGLE, BURBLE ZOMMERBLOT!

ZLUM POODLEDEK, JA WOHL?

Caligula, the previous Emperor, had also tried to invade Britain, but he got no further than the English Channel because his troops were frightened off by the sea. He also made a few raids into Germany and used these as an excuse for a triumph. For his triumph, Caligula paraded some slaves with their hair dyed so that they looked like Germans. They were trained to mutter to each other in German as if they were German prisoners!

In a triumphal procession, magistrates and senators walked at the head, followed by white oxen for sacrifice and wagons loaded with booty taken from the enemy. Next came the prisoners of war, some carried shoulder high on platforms, ready for execution or slavery. The general, in this case Claudius, rode in a gilded chariot, wearing a laurel wreath and carrying a sceptre and an olive branch, the symbol of peace and plenty. Last came the soldiers carrying sticks instead of swords. When it was all over they were given a huge feast and a present of money.

> A SLAVE STOOD AT THE GENERAL'S SHOULDER, HOLDING A GOLDEN CROWN OVER HIS HEAD AND WHISPERING CONTINUOUSLY, 'REMEMBER YOU ARE JUST A MAN' SO AS TO STOP HIM BECOMING CONCEITED.

The Latin title *imperator*, originally meaning a general or commander-in-chief, was given to a victorious general by the acclaim of his troops. This is where our words *emperor* and *imperial* come from. In early days, according to the writer Pliny, during a triumph the general's body was painted bright red.

The procession wound its way through the streets of Rome, finally arriving at the temple of Jupiter Optimus, greatest of the Roman gods, where the general offered up the laurel wreath of victory and the white oxen were sacrificed.

Claudius had had his triumph by the time Caratacus was handed over. But Caratacus was put on show in a sort of mini-triumph. He made such a good speech that Claudius spared him from execution. Caratacus is said to have died in Rome in AD 54.

BOOT CAMPS

– OR SHOULD WE SAY SANDAL CAMPS?
THE ROMAN ARMY

POWER PLAY

> HOW DID THE ROMANS BUILD THEIR MIGHTY EMPIRE?

> WITH THE SWORD!

Roman armies were the best armies in the world for nearly a thousand years and no one had a chance against them. Their soldiers were well trained and well disciplined and their weapons were just right for the types of battles they had to fight. Barbarians went down like daisies under a lawnmower.

During the height of the Empire, the Roman armies usually totalled around 400,000 men. The soldiers could march or jog quickly to any trouble spot along well-built roads. 400,000 was enough to control their 45 million subjects and to deal with troublesome barbarians outside their borders, such as the Ancient Britons.

FELIX THE FOOT SOLDIER

Foot soldiers were the core of the army. There were four types: the *hastati* and *princeps* were young men in the prime of life, the *velites* were light skirmishers and the *triarii* were old-timers 👣, looking forward to retirement and marriage after their twenty-five years of service. (Until AD 197 Roman soldiers were not allowed to marry.)

LEGIONNAIRE AROUND AD 50

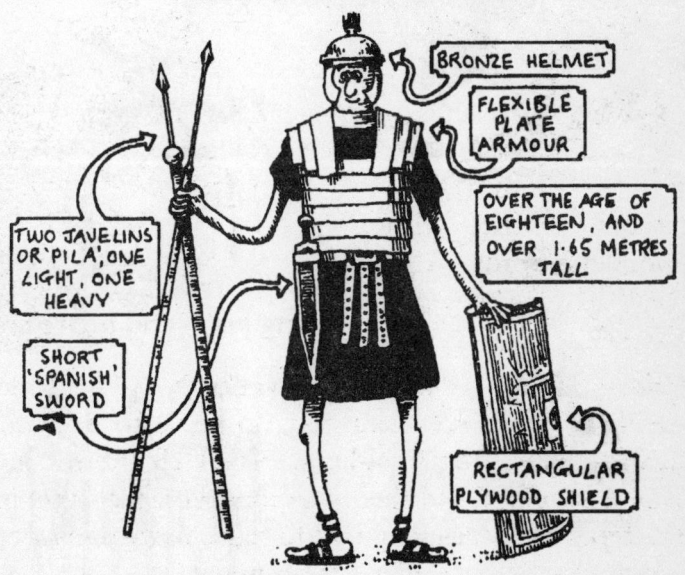

- BRONZE HELMET
- FLEXIBLE PLATE ARMOUR
- OVER THE AGE OF EIGHTEEN, AND OVER 1·65 METRES TALL
- TWO JAVELINS OR 'PILA', ONE LIGHT, ONE HEAVY
- SHORT 'SPANISH' SWORD
- RECTANGULAR PLYWOOD SHIELD

👣 Triarii fought at the back. The Roman saying 'the battle went to the triarii' meant a desperate situation.

👣 The typical Roman sword was copied from a style first used in Spain.

Boot camp

Each soldier was as fit as a fiddle and an expert fighter. They had to practise hard:

Thirty kilometre march with full kit three times a month

General training in stone-slinging, swimming and riding

Sword practice with wooden swords

Long jump and high jump

Vaulting in full armour

Drill once a day (twice during initial training)

When the time came for a battle, the standard tactic was to advance to about twenty metres from the enemy, keeping a space of two metres between each soldier. Then the soldiers would throw their lighter javelins followed by the heavier. The javelins often stuck in the enemies' shields. They had a barbed point which was difficult to pull out, and the metal shaft below the tip was thin so that it bent on impact, making it useless to throw back.

Close up, the soldiers went to work with their swords, frequently dropping to one knee and holding their shields above them while striking upwards. Great big Celts with long swords used to find this technique difficult to fight against.

Ancient battles were incredibly bloody affairs. Imagine a slaughter of say eighty thousand men (the number is nothing out of the ordinary) as happened at the defeat of one British army, all killed by stabbing or slashing 🦶. An adult man has about five litres of blood. That makes up to 400,000 litres of blood swashing around on the battlefield - enough to fill a fair sized lake!

🦶 During the revolt of Boudicca. More of that later.

GOING BALLISTIC

Not all fighting was hand to hand. The Romans had long distance weapons as well. Especially useful were two types of catapult:

The *catapulta* was a bit like a giant crossbow with springs of twisted sinew.

The *ballista* threw stones. Giant ballistas could throw stones of up to forty-five kilograms. They were the heavy artillery of the ancient world.

FOLLOW THE EAGLE!

The soldiers were organised into units of about eighty men, called *centuries*. Six centuries made a *cohort* and ten cohorts together with about 120 despatch riders made a *legion*. At the height of the Empire there were twenty-eight Roman legions and the rest of the army was recruited from *auxiliary* forces made up of men from other nations. Normal battle array was two Roman legions in the centre, flanked by two auxiliary legions, with horse soldiers, or *cavalry*, on the wings.

It is commonly thought that centuries originally contained a hundred soldiers. The Latin word *centum* means a hundred.

OFFICER MATERIAL

Tribunes were aristocratic staff officers, often not very experienced.

The *Legatus* was the commander of a legion.

Centurions commanded centuries.

HANDLE FOR PULLING STANDARD OUT OF THE GROUND

The eagle was the standard of the legion. Loss of the eagle to an enemy was a major disgrace. It was carried by an officer called an *aquilifer*.

As well as officers, legions needed scouts, despatch riders, catapult makers, water engineers, medical orderlies and a master builder.

DO AS YOU'RE TOLD OR ELSE!

Centurions were assisted by standard bearers, trumpeters and a *tessarius*, an officer who received the camp password at night. Long-serving centurions were the backbone of the army. Many spent more than forty years in the service 🦶 , but they were often brutal and corrupt. They carried a vine cane to keep discipline.

I'LL DECIMATE YOU!

Discipline was strict. Deserters and sentries who left their posts were executed. There were even generals who executed their own sons for disobedience. But *decimation* 🦶 was the worst punishment. During a decimation, every tenth man of an offending cohort was clubbed or stoned to death by the men of another cohort. The rest of the decimated cohort had to eat only barley and might have to sleep outside the camp at night for the period of their disgrace.

🦶 One centurion is recorded as having spent sixty-one years in the army.

🦶 *Decimus* is Latin for tenth.

TIME TO MOVE

Roman soldiers had to carry all their own vital supplies - no wonder they were known as 'Marius' mules', after the famous general who first made them carry their own baggage around 106 BC.

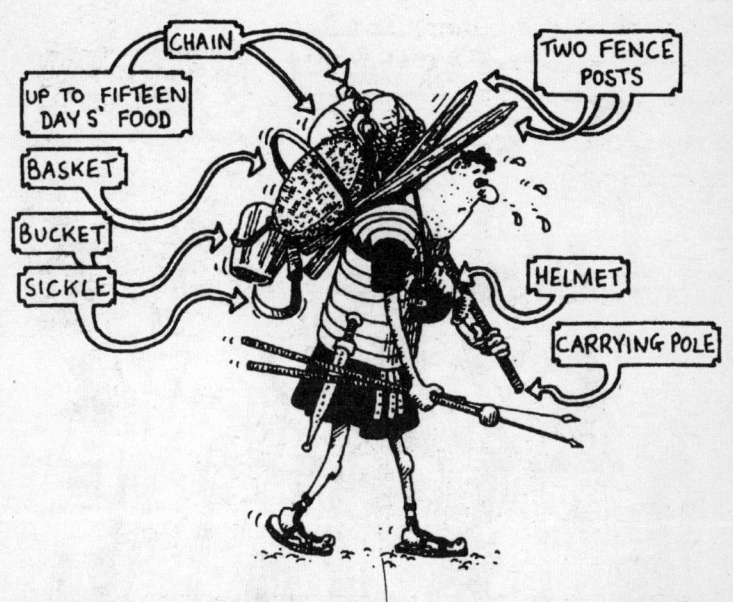

There was a real mule for every eight men. The mule carried their shared tent and any surplus items. In hostile territory the legions marched in battle order with their baggage mules and other equipment protected between the columns of soldiers.

LET'S GO CAMPING

There were no ready-made campsites for Roman soldiers, no shower facilities and no camper vans. Having marched perhaps thirty kilometres, or even as many as fifty, the tired soldiers were not allowed to rest until they had built a fortified camp.

> IT'S ALL RIGHT FOR SOME

> I COULD DO WITH A CUPPA WINE.

Half the army dug a square ditch and mud rampart, while the other half stood guard in battle array. The fence posts they had carried with them were hammered into the top of the rampart and joined with links of chain. Then after the positions of the various tents had been marked out, the baggage train was led into the fortified area and the legion could start to relax. Camps were always laid out in exactly the same way so there was never any danger of getting lost.

There were no gates on temporary camps. But permanent camps not only had gates, they had stone walls and some, the legionary bases, stayed in the same place for hundreds of years. Several English towns such as Chester and Cirencester grew up around Roman camps.

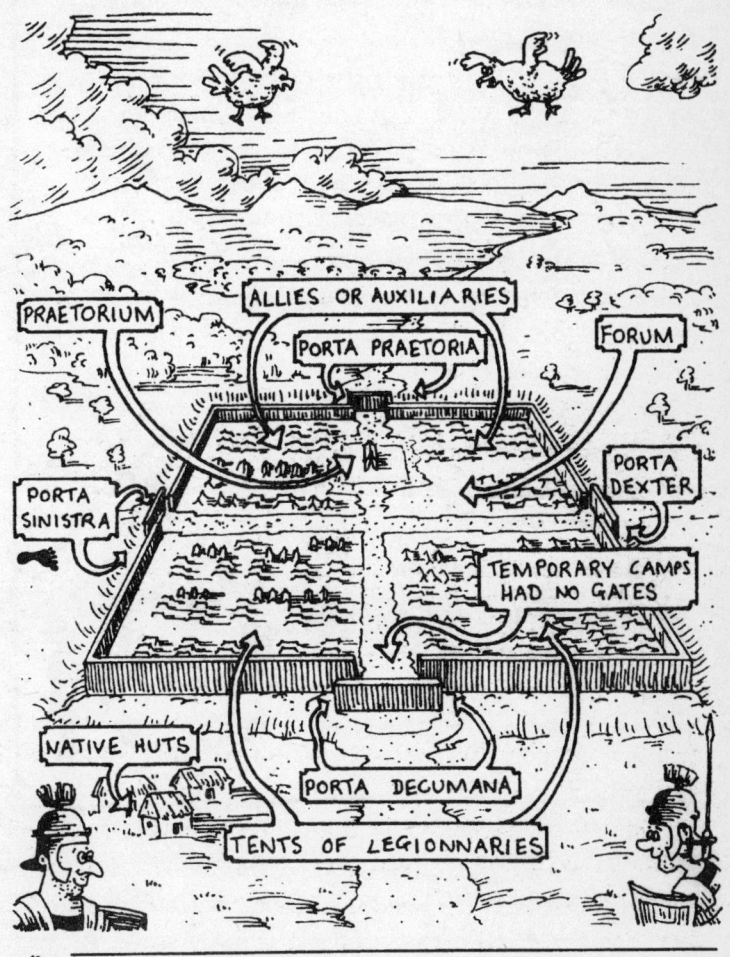

Porta means gate in latin. *Sinister* means left and *dexter* means right. The *praetorium* was the camp heaquarters, so the *porta praetoria* was the gate of the headquarters. The *porta decumana* was the main gate.

STRAP UP YOUR SANDALS

COULD *YOU* BE A ROMAN? (PART 1)

You are applying for a job as Roman general. You must answer the following questions correctly. (Answers on page 122)

1 A legion must keep fit. What are your orders for the legionnaires?

a A sauna with massage twice daily
b A thirty kilometre march with full kit three times a month
c Sword practice with sharpened swords

2 What are the triarii?
a Old soldiers who fight at the back
b Soldiers who try extra hard
c Three-pointed spears

3 How large is a legion?
a 3 metres tall and about five round the middle
b Approximately 400 men
c Approximately 5,000 men

THEY CAME, THEY SAW, THEY TOOK

ROADS, WALLS AND THINGS IN BETWEEN

> Having conquered half of England, we Romans were ready to enjoy it.

TIME FOR A BREATHER

The Romans lost no time in rebuilding Camulodunum (Colchester), the largest Celtic town in Britain, as a town for retired legionnaires. Such towns were called *colonies*. Soon there was a massive temple to the Emperor Claudius just outside the town boundaries.

Britain in AD 60

- BRIGANTES – FAIRLY FRIENDLY TO ROME
- BARBARIANS
- COLCHESTER (CAMULODUNUM)
- ST. ALBANS (VERULAMIUM)
- UNDER ROMAN CONTROL
- LONDON

And it was all paid for by taxes from local people.

Everything was going brilliantly for the Romans, apart from a few problems with troublesome Celts in the north and in Wales. The governor withdrew most of the legions from southern England.

Roman emperors were worshipped as gods. More about that later.

Roman mistake No.1 - destroying the Druids

The Druids had many strange and frightening rituals. They made sacrifices in groves of sacred trees, where every tree was 'sprinkled with human gore', according to descriptions by the Roman writer Tacitus. They are said to have built huge hollow figures of men out of sticks then crammed these 'wicker men' full of human prisoners before setting fire to them. They cut magic mistletoe with golden sickles and even ate deadly nightshade to give themselves visions. And they disapproved of reading and writing, which is why we know so little about them.

The headquarters of all the Druids in Europe was on the island of Anglesey off the north coast of Wales. Safe on their island they continued their sacred rituals.

Romans thought the Druids were disgusting. What they found really disgusting was that the Druids encouraged people to fight the Romans.

Being Romans, the Romans set out to crush the Druids. They attacked Anglesey.

Deadly nightshade is an extremely poisonous plant. The berries will often kill whoever eats them.

We have a description of the scene before the battle by a Roman general later to become Emperor Agricola:

'The enemy lined the shore in a dense armed mass. Among them black-robed women with dishevelled hair like furies, brandishing torches. Close by stood Druids raising their hands to heaven and screaming dreadful curses. This weird sight awed the Romans into a kind of paralysis ...'

But not for long. The Romans attacked and won. They chopped down the sacred groves and slaughtered the Britons. Then almost at the moment of victory their commander, the governor Suetonius Paulinus, received a message of far worse trouble in the south ...

ROMAN MISTAKE No.2 (A BIG MISTAKE) – BUGGING BOUDICCA

Boudicca, Queen of the Iceni, was a huge woman with a harsh voice and a mass of red hair which fell to her knees. She was terrifying, and she despised Roman men 'if these can indeed be called men who bathe in warm water, eat delicacies ... and sleep on soft couches'. Unfortunately for everyone it seems that the Romans didn't notice her attitude.

When Boudicca's husband King Prasutagus died in AD 59 or 60, the Romans beat Boudicca and tried to take her kingdom from her. Boudicca was not the sort of woman to accept this treatment meekly. She started a mass rebellion of British warriors.

The Romans were caught on the hop because their army was in Anglesey dealing with the Druids. By the time the legions had marched south again, Boudicca's followers had sacked Colchester, London and St Albans, taking no prisoners, selling no slaves and killing up to seventy thousand Romans. There is still a layer of ash beneath the streets of the City of London from the time of Boudicca's attack.

The main Roman legions hurried south in forced marches along a newly-built road known as Watling Street 🐾. They were too late to stop the destruction but they finally defeated Boudicca in a battle in the Midlands 🐾. The British had brought their wives and children to watch the battle from a sort of wagon park behind their main army. But there was nothing to watch except slaughter. About eighty thousand tribesmen and four hundred Romans lost their lives. Boudicca escaped but probably poisoned herself soon afterwards. Thus ended the largest ever British rebellion against the Romans.

🐾 The modern A5 follows the route of Watling Street.

🐾 The battlefield was probably at Mancetter (near Atherston) on the A5, where there is now a stone quarry.

LOADS OF ROADS

Boudicca was beaten by Roman roads almost as much as by Roman soldiers. It was the roads which allowed Suetonius Paulinus to gather his forces quickly for the counter-attack.

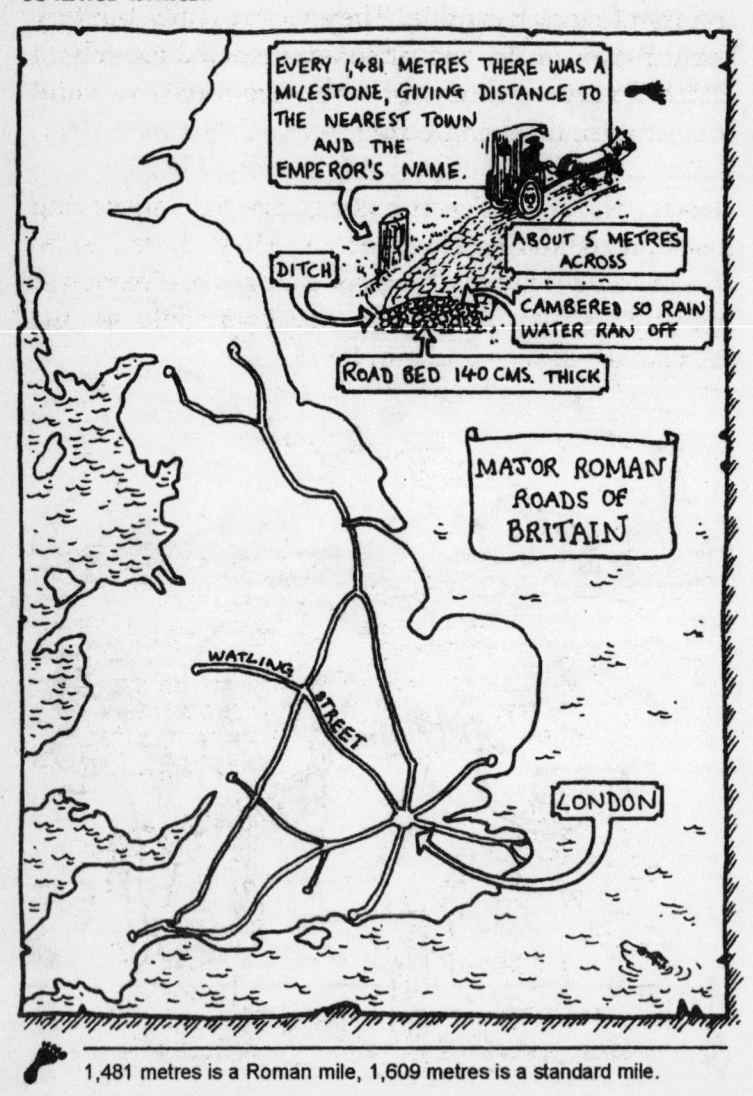

EVERY 1,481 METRES THERE WAS A MILESTONE, GIVING DISTANCE TO THE NEAREST TOWN AND THE EMPEROR'S NAME.

ABOUT 5 METRES ACROSS

DITCH

CAMBERED SO RAIN WATER RAN OFF

ROAD BED 140 CMS. THICK

MAJOR ROMAN ROADS OF BRITAIN

WATLING STREET

LONDON

1,481 metres is a Roman mile, 1,609 metres is a standard mile.

The first Roman roads in Britain would have been made quickly and would not have lasted long in British weather, but they were soon replaced by roads which were seriously Roman and seriously permanent. An average Roman road contained 20,000 tonnes of stone per mile. They were mainly built by the army, but slaves and prisoners helped them - about 40,000 British prisoners of war were forced to build roads in neighbouring Gaul.

Roads were laid out using special surveying instruments and smoke beacons. They tended to be laid in straight lines with major changes of direction at high points from which the surveyors could see the next smoke beacon and aim for it.

85,000 kilometres of roads criss-crossed the Empire. There was a saying: 'All roads lead to Rome' which in a sense they all did, since that's where all the orders came from. Imperial messengers could travel at speed on relays of horses kept at intervals of ten to twenty kilometres, carrying the Emperor's edicts to the furthest corners of his empire - such as Britain.

TALL WALLS

In the north of Britain the roads fizzled out. The Romans never conquered all of Scotland. It was full of savages, and anyway there was nothing there worth grabbing.

Instead they built a wall to keep the savages out. It's called Hadrian's Wall after the emperor who ordered it built and you can still see bits of it. It was the largest structure ever built by the Romans, which is saying quite a lot. It took ten years to build .

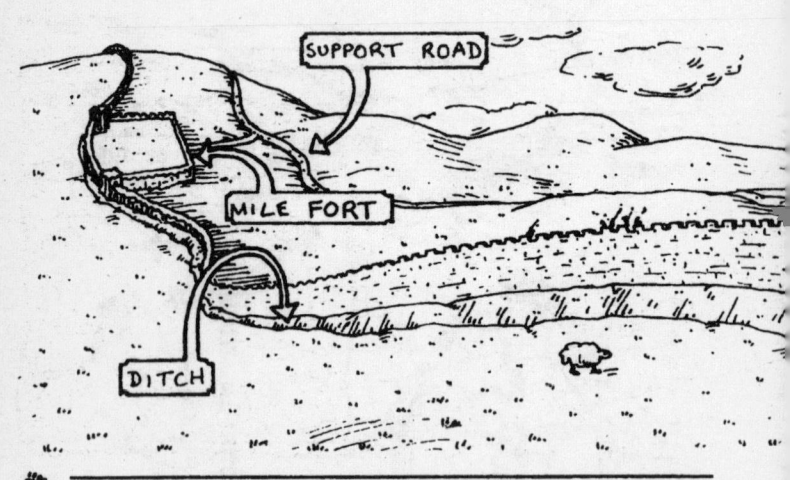

In AD 142, another wall, called the Antonine Wall, was built in Scotland, between the Firths of Forth and Clyde, but it was abandoned in AD 196. It was ordered by the emperor Antoninus Pius.

Hadrian's Wall stretched 120 kilometres from Bowness in the west to Wallsend in the east, right across the north of England. It was wide enough for a chariot to ride on top of it, and along its length were sixteen large forts with smaller forts every Roman mile, together with signalling turrets. There was a hospital in every fortress and in most of the forts.

The wall was manned by soldiers from all over the Empire. We know this from tombstones and other objects which they left behind. For instance, some cavalry from Germany known as 'Notfrieds Irregulars' were stationed at Housesteads ◂ in the centre of the wall and a unit of Africans was stationed at Burgh-by-Sands in the west. The soldiers did a good job. In all the time the wall was in use (from AD 122-383) it was only once overrun.

Roman name *Borocovicium*.

Brain Bruiser

Could *you* be a Roman? (Part 2)

Romans used letters for numbers: I = 1, V = 5, X = 10, L = 50, C = 100, D = 500, M = 1000. The numbers in between were made up of two or more of these letters. These were normally added together. For instance III = 3, VI = 6, XVI = 16. However, if a number was smaller than the one immediately after it, it was subtracted from that number, e.g. IV = 4, IXX = 19, XLIV = 44.

The following are the Roman numbers from 1 to 20: I, II, III, IV, V VI, VII, VIII, IX, X, XI, XII, XIII, XIV, XV, XVI, XVII, XVIII, IXX, XX

Can you work out what these numbers are? (Answers on page 122.)

a XXIII
b XLVII
c CLXXIV

SLAVES AND LADDERS

THE SOCIAL LADDER, FROM SLAVES TO EMPERORS WITH RUNGS IN BETWEEN

For nearly four hundred years Britain was a small province on the edge of a mighty empire. The governors who ruled it were appointed by the Emperor in Rome and society was organised along Roman lines.

POWER PYRAMID

EMPEROR

GOVERNORS AND OTHER TOP OFFICIALS (USUALLY ROMAN NOBLES)

KNIGHTS

FREEDMEN

SLAVES

EMPERORS MADE EASY – A BIT OF BACKGROUND

Once upon a time Rome was a republic: it had no monarch and the leader, or rather leaders, were elected. Every year the nobles voted for two *consuls* who had day to day charge of running things and ran the senate, which was a bit like parliament. Then along came Julius Caesar and everything changed.

'Caesar' meant 'head of hair', which is strange because both Julius and Augustus, the next 'Caesar' (as all the emperors came to be called), were bald. Julius took all power in Rome into his own hands. From that time on Rome was always ruled by one or two powerful men who came to be given titles such as *Caesar*, *Augustus* and *Imperator*, meaning emperor, by the senate. Julius was stabbed to death on the Ides of March (15 March) 44 BC by a bunch of conspirators who thought he had grown too powerful.

> The Romans counted dates from three fixed points in each month: *Kalends*, *Nones* and *Ides*, so a day was said to be so many days before or after one of these fixed days or actually on a fixed day.

GREAT DATES

Julius changed the Roman world, and he also changed the calendar. The old Roman calendar had only ten months with a period in winter without any months, March being the first month of the year. (The extra months of January and February were added later, which is why September, which comes from the Latin word *septum* meaning 'seventh' is now the ninth month.) The months were too short, so that each year started earlier than the year before. Julius sorted things out. The months of the year as we know them today are almost the same as on Julius' Roman calendar.

January - called after Janus, god of beginnings and doorways among other things
February - after a Roman feast of purification
March - the first month of the year until 153 BC, after Mars, god of war and originally agriculture
April - probably after Aphrodite, Greek goddess of love
May - called after the Roman goddess Maia
June - means sacred to the goddess Juno
July - called after Julius Caesar, used to be called Quintilis - the fifth month (from mid-March)
August - called after the Emperor Augustus, used to be called Sextilis - the sixth month
September - the seventh month
October - from the Latin *octo* meaning eight
November - from the Latin *novem* meaning nine
December - from the Latin *decem* meaning ten

CLEOPATRA
A CLASSY ACT

In 48 BC Queen Cleopatra of Egypt was eighteen years old. At that time Caesar had come to Egypt with a large army to defeat another powerful Roman called Pompey. Cleopatra had herself wrapped up in a carpet and smuggled into Caesar's presence. Almost as soon as he saw her, Caesar fell in love with her and soon took her to Rome.

After Caesar's murder, Cleopatra and Caesar's young friend, Marcus Antonius, also fell madly in love. Unfortunately, Antony and Cleopatra were defeated in a civil war by the next Emperor, a short, balding young man called Octavianus, later called Augustus, who was Caesar's heir. Captured by Octavianus, Cleopatra tried to charm him as well but failed.

She killed herself with a bite from a poisonous snake called an asp. She already knew about asps from experiments on live human beings.

LET'S TRY AN ASP ON THIS ONE.

On your guard!

Each emperor was protected by a special regiment of several thousand soldiers known as the *Praetorian Guard*. They were paid three-and-a-half times as much as ordinary legionnaires, wore a special old-fashioned uniform and were the only soldiers permanently stationed in Rome.

Praetorians were meant to protect emperors, but they often killed them instead. When new emperors came to power, they used to give the Praetorians a special bonus worth up to five years' pay - really a bribe to keep them sweet. No bribe could mean no emperor - and often did! It was officers of the Praetorian Guard who murdered Caligula, the mad emperor who ruled before Claudius.

POSH TOFFS AND POOR PLEBS

Top of the Roman toffs were the *patricians*. Usually the governor of Britain was a patrician appointed by the emperor. They were aristocrats. They sat in the Senate, lived in beautiful houses in Rome and often thought themselves superior to the emperor himself, who in later years was often not an aristocrat.

All other Romans were known as *plebeians* or *plebs* for short. In the early years of Rome they had no rights and were forbidden to marry patricians or to hold important jobs. Later they got their own assembly led by *tribunes* and won the right to hold important jobs. Eventually it was impossible to tell a patrician from a rich pleb.

Knights were rich plebs and became a separate middle class. The second most important man in Britain after the governor was the *procurator* who was always a knight. He looked after tax collection and the emperor's mines and estates.

NERO
A MAD EMPEROR STORY

Nero (AD 37-68) didn't like Britain. He thought it was cold and wet. (The fact that Boudicca's rebellion happened during his reign can't have helped.)

He also didn't like his mother. Having decided to get rid of her, he persuaded Mum to board a special boat during a parade of ships. Little did Mum know that the boat was specially designed to let in water and its roof was designed to lower as the water rushed in, thus crushing those inside. Unfortunately Nero's evil scheme backfired. Mum escaped and swam to safety in front of a large crowd.

Nero had to have her murdered by a soldier instead.

SLAVE GRADES

Slaves were bottom of the heap in Roman Britain. They were the property of their owners who could do what they wanted with them. However, some slaves had quite important jobs. The first British civil servant whose name we know was a slave named Anencletus. He worked for the London city council's staff, perhaps as a secretary.

I'M BUSY FILING - CAN'T HELP YOU I'M AFRAID.

In fact nearly all work in the Roman Empire was done by slaves. Slaves worked the farms and mines, there were slave doctors and dentists and secretaries like Anencletus. Slave labour became a habit: in Rome itself none of the free citizens were prepared to labour. They were supported by supplies of food and drink given out by the government and the produce of their slaves if they owned any.

WORK? WHAT'S THAT?

Anencletus is Greek for 'blameless'.

In the later years of the Empire there was six months' holiday per year anyway. But not for slaves!

WAVES OF SLAVES

With each new conquest, more slaves flooded on to the Roman slave markets. After the Romans conquered Sardinia there was such a glut of Sardinian slaves that 'cheap as a Sardinian' became a common saying. An ordinary slave was cheaper than a horse or even a cow. You could pick them up for 500 denarii - a horse would cost you much more. In the slave market on the Greek island of Delos, ten thousand slaves might be sold on the same day. There would have been thousands of British slaves of both sexes for sale after the Roman invasion. Later, when the conquests stopped, the supply of new slaves dried up and they became more expensive.

The number of slaves was a constant worry to the government. In Italy there were three slaves to every free person. In Britain the number of slaves compared to freemen would have been less, but even so there would have been a great many. Slaves weren't allowed to wear uniforms in case they saw how they outnumbered the free people and then rebelled.

SPARTACUS
A SAD STORY

Spartacus was a deserter from the army who was arrested and forced to train as a slave gladiator. In 73 BC he led a break-out of around seventy gladiators from the gladiator school at Capua. They hid on Mount Vesuvius and when besieged on the mountain they escaped down ladders made of wild vines. Soon other escaped slaves flocked to join them. By the following year Spartacus commanded an army of 90,000 men.

Spartacus defeated several Roman armies, but his men had no discipline. They started to behave like criminals, murdering, looting and attacking whenever they could. He realized that such a rabble was no longer able to fight properly and pleaded with them to escape with him from Italy. His men refused - they were having too much of a good time!

When Roman billionaire Crassus led yet another army against them in 71 BC, the escaped slaves fought bravely but were defeated. Spartacus was killed and six thousand of his men were crucified along the main road to Rome from the south.

Crucifixion was a painful form of punishment reserved for slaves and the worst criminals. The victim was either nailed or tied to a wooden cross and left to die. It was an unusual method of execution for a free man such as Jesus Christ, who was crucified in AD 33.

SLAVE YOURSELF THE BOTHER

Slaves were so cheap at the height of the Empire that rich people owned hundreds or even thousands of them. Some owners couldn't do anything for themselves:

ONE MINUTE PAST TWO, TWO MINUTES PAST TWO, THREE...

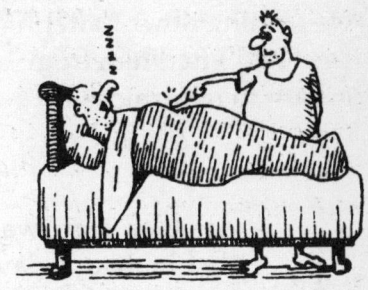

Slaves reminded them to go to bed at night and woke them in the morning.

'Human clock' slaves called out the time.

THIS IS PETRONIUS, MASTER — ERR, OR WAS IT PUBLIUS.

Some slaves did nothing but stand around and look good.

Nomenclatores remembered the names of visitors.

Slaves did everything for their owners. They bathed them, combed their hair and got them dressed. The writer Seneca describes one man as asking: 'Am I sitting down?' after his slaves had lifted him from the bath to his armchair.

Another man was so unused to walking that he had a slave walk before him when he did, to point out any bumps in the road and to remind his master not to walk into things. There were even slaves to do their owners' thinking: one man had a slave to stand behind his chair at dinner parties and tell him clever things to say.

It was fashionable for dinner guests to dry their hands in slaves' hair.

Household slaves might be pampered like favourite pets, but others were not so lucky. Some Roman farms in Britain have been found with special underground prisons with chains where the farm workers were kept at night. One rich Roman woman reckoned it was cheaper to work her slaves to death and then to get new ones than to feed them properly.

It wasn't all bad. Every December at Saturnalia, the festival of the god Saturn, the tables were turned and slaves were waited on by their masters. Christians replaced Saturnalia with a new winter festival - Christmas.

To free or not to free

Slavery is one of the hardest things for us to understand about the Romans. How could they believe that a slave was just a 'tame animal', and also that the same slave became a human being immediately he or she was freed? And if slaves *were* no better than animals, how come so many were freed? After all you're unlikely to free a real animal such as a cow. The writer Cicero reckoned that on average a slave would be freed after only six years of slavery, though he may have been exaggerating.

The lowest age at which a slave was allowed to be free was thirty. Many were freed as soon as they reached that age. Others might save up their *peculium* and buy themselves from their owners. Many more were freed at the death of their owners, and a lucky handful even inherited their owners' property. There were so many ex-slaves and the children of ex-slaves that it's reckoned that everyone in Rome had at least one slave ancestor, even the aristocrats.

> YOU SAY YOU'RE DESCENDED FROM FELIX SLAVONICUS — FUNNY SORT OF NAME, ISN'T IT?

IT'S THE LAW, CITIZENS!

The first Roman laws were very tough. They gave a lot of authority to the male head of the family, known as the *paterfamilias*. Fathers could and sometimes did execute their children if they committed certain crimes. However things softened as the years went by, until by the end there were even laws to protect slaves, and slaves could no longer be killed by their owners without 'good' reason.

> THIS IS FOR YOUR OWN GOOD, CORNELIUS.

The *peculium* was money a slave managed to save for him or herself from tips and other small payments.

The first Roman laws were made in 753 BC and the last in the west in AD 535. Being Roman laws, they were all efficiently written down. There was no shortage; by the end there were three million judgements written out in twenty-six volumes! Roman law is still the basis for most law in Europe.

At first, the only people having full rights and duties under the law were the *paterfamilias* or heads of families. These were the first Roman citizens. Only citizens could use Roman law courts or appeal to the Emperor in Rome. Even as the Empire expanded, everyone else had to make do with local laws, which were different in different places. But ex-legionnaires became citizens automatically on retirement, and gradually, by this and other means, citizenship was given to most of the people of Italy and to some in places beyond. Saint Paul, one of the founders of Christianity, was a Roman citizen even though he was Jewish. Finally in AD 212 Emperor Caracalla gave citizenship to almost all the free inhabitants of the Empire, including the Romano-Britons.

The Ancient Britons had been changed from spiky-haired, blue-painted savages into citizens of the most powerful Empire on Earth in just 150 years from the time of their defeat by Claudius' army.

Or so it seemed ...

He was born in Gaul and used to wear a hooded tunic called a *caracalla*, which is why he's always called Caracalla. His real name was *Marcus Aurelius Antoninus*.

NITTY GRITTY CITIES

FANCY FORUMS AND BUSY BASILICAS

THE THREE Cs

Cities go with civilization like tomatoes go with ketchup. In fact, our words *citizen*, *city* and *civilization* all come from the Latin word for a city: *civitas*. Before the Romans there were no cities in Britain - and no civilization in the way of books, laws, paintings, home comforts and things like that. The best the Ancient Britons could manage was the odd scruffy collection of huts around the big hut of the local king or queen.

The Romans lost no time in changing all that. Towns sprang up like dandelions on a cabbage patch. You can hardly move in England without bumping into towns started by the Romans.

> If the name of your town ends in 'eter' 'cester' or 'chester', 'caistor' 'caister' 'cetter' or 'caster', like Exeter, Gloucester and Chester, you can be sure that it was started by the Romans. All these word endings come originally from the Latin word *castor*, meaning a military camp.

A Roman's home is Rome

It's no wonder the Romans built cities. After all, Rome was a city before it became the head of an Empire as well. And it was the largest city in the world. Rome had the greatest temples, the greatest theatres, the greatest circuses and amphitheatres. Water was brought from far outside the town on the greatest aqueducts. Cities throughout the Empire copied it.

THE SEVEN HILLS OF ROME
- QUIRINALE
- VIMINAL
- CAPITOLINE
- ESQUILINE
- PALATINE
- CAELIUS
- AVENTINE

RIVER TIBER

It's reckoned that at the time of the great fire of AD 64 *two million* people lived there. That meant two million Romans to be fed, watered and kept happy without any of the modern technology we take for granted, such as computers, cars and television. Despite the lack of technology, in many ways it was quite like a modern city. It even had traffic jams: heavy

---

Circuses and ampitheatres were a bit like football stadiums today. They were where people went to watch horse races and other more gruesome games. More on that later.

The citizens blamed Nero for the fire. He is said to have played his lyre as the flames roared through the city. Nero in turn blamed the early Christians for starting it.

goods wagons were only allowed into the city at night so as to reduce traffic. People complained that the noise of wooden wheels on the streets paved with dark grey rock was deafening.

Old soldiers' homes

The first cities in Britain were built by soldiers who had retired from the Roman army. When they started their three *colonies* 🐾 at Colchester, Gloucester and Lincoln 🐾 they made sure the temples and other public buildings were in the Roman style, to make a real home from home. The houses were often built within old army camps as at Colchester, so being old soldiers no doubt they felt doubly at home.

🐾 See page 35, *colonies* were settlements of retired Roman soldiers.

🐾 'Lincoln' is short for *Lindum Colonium*, meaning a *colony* in *Lindum* (roughly modern Lincolnshire).

Emperors liked colonies because the old soldiers showed the natives how to live a civilized life the Roman way, and Emperors wanted everyone to become Roman or to 'wear the toga' as Julius Caesar put it. Once in their new homes, the old codgers settled down to farm - on land that had recently belonged to the defeated Britons.

New towns were built by the recently-defeated Britons as well. They took longer to get started than the Romans because they didn't have experience of building, except for huts and hill-forts. The Romans helped out by lending military engineers, so the new British-built towns also looked a bit like army barracks. The first two were Canterbury and St Albans.

Later, London (known as *Augustus* for a long time) grew to be the largest town and the city of Bath, known to the Romans as *Aquae Sulis*, was the poshest because Romano-Britons went there to relax in the natural hot springs. You can still see the remains of the Roman baths at Bath.

The *toga* was the standard Roman garment. More about that later.

Consentius's classical contours

Consentius the classical architect has designed a classical 🦶 temple. Unfortunately, he drank too much sweet Greek wine the night before and he's drawn everything in the wrong place. Can you help him sort it out?

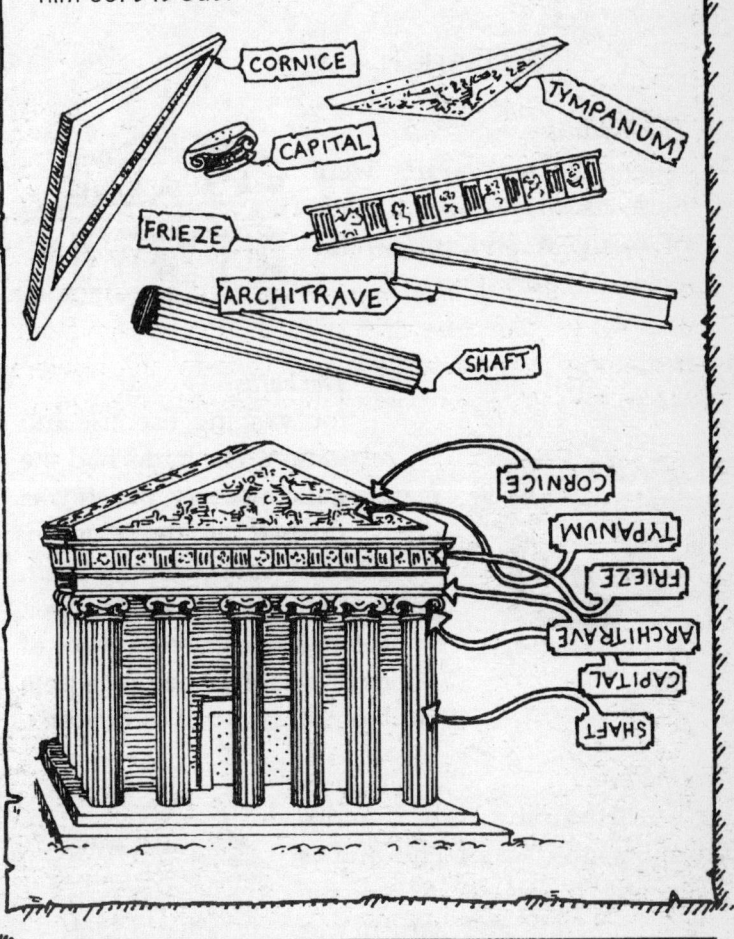

> The word *classical* means, among other things, 'of Ancient Greek or Roman culture'.

WHY BUILD FORUMS FOR'EM?

The centre of every large town was similar to the centre of Rome. Each one had a *forum*, a central area where people met to discuss business and where the market was held. Most of the major public buildings were grouped around it, and there would be covered shops and arcades either around the forum or in the nearby streets.

PUBLIC PLACES

The basilica
where the law courts were held, and also used as a place of business and offices for the local council.

The baths
for washing, exercise and relaxation. The baths had the main public lavatory, which was flushed into the sewer by outflow water from the main pools. There was no toilet paper. Toilet-users shared a piece of cloth or a sponge tied on a pole and kept in a tub of salty water.

Temples
for worshipping gods, but also used to store documents and as meeting places. In Rome, the temple of the god Saturn was the State Treasury.

Amphitheatre
where shows were put on.

MAJESTIC MOMENT

COULD *YOU* BE A ROMAN? (PART 3)

Consentius the architect has drunk too much wine again. He's been causing a nuisance and has to go to court. You are the magistrate. Where would you find your court room? (Answer on page 122)

a   In the temple of Saturn
b   Above a wine shop at the back of the forum
c   In the basilica

HOME TRUTHS

The rich often had a large town house, or *domus*, as well as a villa in the country. The *domus* of a patrician was normally a large inward looking building, perhaps with shops set in the outside walls. There were plenty of rooms, and husband and wife had separate bedrooms (slaves were usually crammed into small rooms in the cellar). The houses of the rich had their own central heating and indoor toilet. In fact, an indoor toilet was something to boast about as an expensive car might be today.

Things were different for the poor. In Rome and in many other towns the majority of the population lived in blocks of flats called *insulae*. The cheapest flats were at the top where, in Rome at least, cooking was forbidden for fear of fires. There were no toilets. If you needed the toilet, you had to find a public toilet - or throw muck into the street.

'*Cave*' means 'beware'.

DRUSILLA'S VILLA

LIFE IN THE COUNTRY

Drusilla has just got married. She's about to move into her husband's new *villa*.

HUT OR VILLA?

Cities may have been necessary for civilization, but most British people lived on small farms and spoke Celtic for the whole time that the Romans ruled Britain.

But gradually rich farmers started to build *villas*, which is Latin for 'country houses'. Villas were as different from Celtic huts as the Tower of London is from a bouncy castle. They were solidly built with plenty of rooms and they had all the Roman comforts such as central heating.

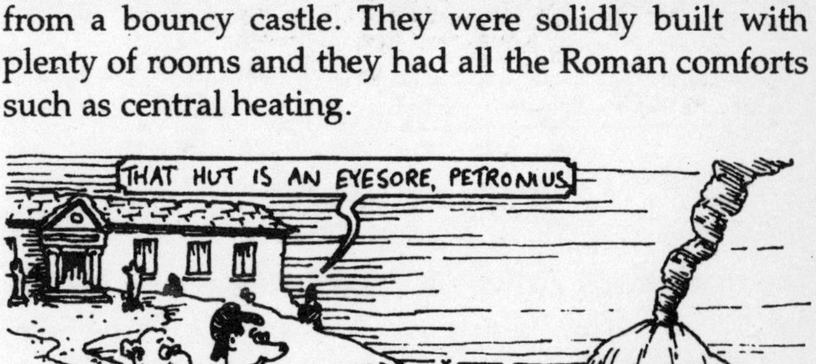

HERE IT IS - DRUSILLA'S VILLA

Drusilla's fiancé is a rich Romano-Briton called Didius. He's just built this amazing new villa for them to live in together.

MOSAIC FLOORS

DINING ROOMS AND RECEPTION ROOMS

SLATE OR TILE ROOF

STONE FOUNDATIONS

BOX HEDGES AROUND PATHS

The main crops grown on British villa estates would have been barley, wheat and beans, but villa owners

> Mosaics are pictures or patterns made up of lots of small pieces of different coloured stone.

aimed to be self-sufficient in almost everything. They even grew their own wine - when they were allowed to.

Labels on illustration:
- FIRE FOR HEATING HYPOCAUST
- BATH HOUSE
- KITCHENS
- SEPARATE BUILDINGS FOR SLAVES, ANIMALS AND HIRED WORKERS
- MOST VILLAS WERE BUILT NEAR TO ROADS.

In the first century AD so much land throughout the Empire was given over to producing wine instead of wheat that the Emperor Domitian forbade all wine-growing outside Italy. It was only in the third century that the British were allowed to grow wine again.

A *hypocaust* was a central heating system. Normally hot air was circulated under the floor.

DRUSILLA'S MARRIAGE

Drusilla and Didius have decided to get married in Roman style. Drusilla did not choose her own husband. Parents chose who their children should marry, as in some Eastern cultures today.

The night before the marriage Drusilla left her toys and young maiden's clothes in the care of the household gods 👣 to show that she was now an adult woman.

Next day she wore a white wool tunic, orange shoes, a short orange veil and put a wreath of the herb marjoram on her head.

Then the bridegroom came to her house for the ceremony and a feast.

Later the happy couple walked in a procession to their new house, chanting marriage hymns to the gods.

👣 Called *lares*. More on these later.

Once they got to the villa, Drusilla rubbed oil and fat on the doorposts and wound wool round them in a traditional Roman ceremony. Then Didius carried her over the threshold.

KIDS' STUFF

Once they were married, a young couple would expect to have children, but sadly not many of those children would grow up to become adults. The British gravestone of one centurion's wife, aged only twenty-seven at the time of her death, shows that she had already had seven children and that only one was still alive.

But never mind: surplus children were killed off anyway. The Romans were ruthless - malformed or unwanted children were exposed to die on the hillsides outside Rome from earliest times. The remains of nearly one hundred new-born babies have been found beside a villa at Hambleden in Buckinghamshire.

The children of the poor and of slaves would have had to start work at an early age. But the kids of the rich didn't work and had a wide range of toys to play with. Here are a few of them:

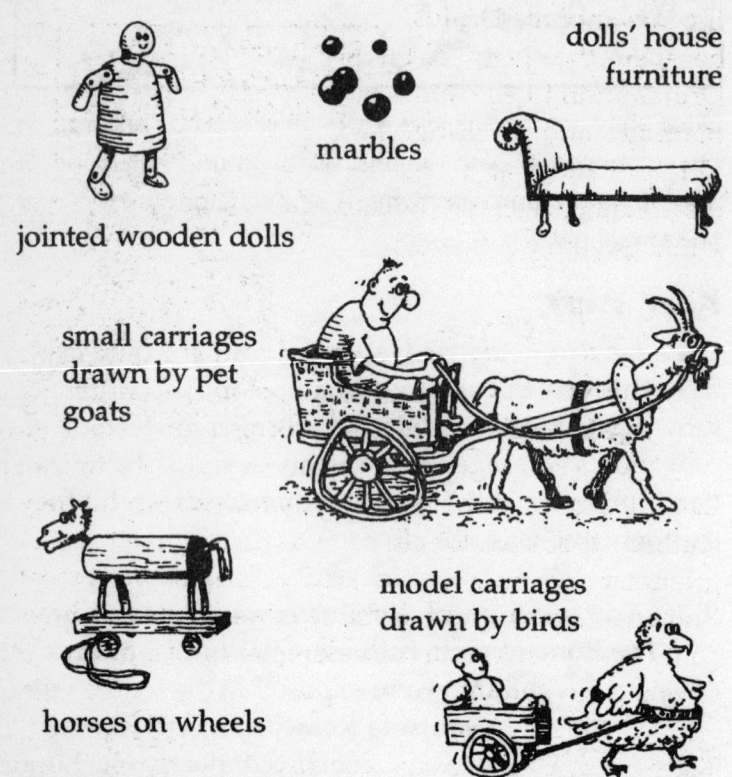

jointed wooden dolls

marbles

dolls' house furniture

small carriages drawn by pet goats

horses on wheels

model carriages drawn by birds

SCHOOL

Both boys and girls went to primary school from the ages of six or seven. The school was often a room close to the forum of the local town. The pupils were taken there by their *pedagogues*, slaves who looked after them and heard them recite their lessons. In the case of Drusilla's children this might have meant a journey of several kilometres there and back each day between the villa and the town.

The main lessons were reading and writing, which was practised either by scratching letters on a wax-coated wooden board or by writing with ink and a reed pen. It was Roman schools that finally killed off the power of the Druids, because the poor old Druids didn't believe in reading and writing. This put them at a big disadvantage when it came to winning young followers.

READING AGAIN, CATARACT? HAND ME THE BOOK, YOU DISMAL BOY!

A DRUID

Later, the boys went on to a *grammaticus* where they studied difficult subjects such as Greek, poetry and grammar under a well-educated teacher. Because most Romano-Britons spoke Celtic at home, Drusilla's boys could have ended up speaking three languages - Greek, Latin and Celtic.

Teachers at the grammaticus had to know their subjects. Because teaching wasn't very well paid, to encourage people to do the job the wages were tax-free. Discipline was harsh and teachers knew how to keep order: several carvings of teachers holding sticks have been found.

Then at fifteen the brightest boys went on to a *rhetor*, a teacher who taught them how to speak in public. This was an important skill in Roman times.

While the bright boys went to the rhetor, at fifteen the girls were ready to get married. Which is where we started this chapter with Drusilla.

THE GOOD LIFE

LIVING IT UP AT BANQUETS, AND OTHER BASHES

> Rich Celts took to the Roman way of life like ducks to water. Who can blame them? With slaves to tend to your every whim, there was plenty of time for the luxuries of life, such as getting ready for dinner.

WE DINE AT NINE

Drusilla and Didius have been invited to dinner in a nearby villa. Dinner started at around four in the afternoon, or the 'ninth hour' as the Romans would have called it, because they didn't number the hours in the same way that we do.

DIDIUS DARLING, THE DINNRI HAVE INVITED US TO DINNER. I'LL BE DARNED IF I'VE GOT ANYTHING DECENT TO WEAR.

FIVE PAST FIVE, SIX PAST FIVE, SEVEN...

A GOOD SCRAPE

Every villa had its own bath house, or several of them. They were smaller versions of the big public baths in the towns. A large villa like Drusilla's would have a room for getting undressed, a room for a cold plunge, a *tepidarium* or warm room and a steam room like a sauna. The Celts used a sort of soap, but if a rich Briton chose to follow the Roman fashion, he or she would be covered in olive oil then scraped clean by a slave using a curved metal instrument called a *strigil*.

GOOD-LOOKING OR WHAT?

It's unlikely the *dominus*, or owner, of a British villa would have paid as much attention to himself as a smooth dresser in Rome. After all, who was he going to meet on a daily basis apart from his wife and children, his slaves and the odd cow? Besides, his poorer neighbours might still be painting themselves with woad 👣 and laugh at him.

But if he was going out to dinner the dominus would probably make an effort. After all, the ancient Greeks and Romans thought that beauty was a virtue, in fact one of the highest virtues 👣. Back in Rome, some men spent a lot of time and money on looking good ...

👣 It was the custom of the Ancient Britons to paint or tattoo themselves with blue dye from the woad plant.

👣 The Emperor Septimus Severus ate hare every day because it was meant to help you stay good looking.

They might paint their faces, including highlights on their skin. If they were going bald, they might wear false hair to cover the bald patch or even paint pretend hair over it! The Emperor Gallienus powdered his hair with gold dust. It's hard to imagine a Romano-British villa-owner going quite so far.

THE MILKY WAY

It wouldn't do to disturb a rich Roman woman while she was sleeping: you might get an unpleasant shock. She might be wearing a *poppaeana*, a face mask invented by Nero's wife Poppaea. The poppaeana was a mixture of dough and asses' milk worn on the face at night to improve the complexion. There was another type of face mask made of rice and beanflour which was meant to remove wrinkles. Face masks were washed off in the morning with a rinse of luke-warm asses' milk.

In fact asses' milk seems to have been the ultimate beauty aid. Cleopatra bathed in it every day. Some women washed their faces in it several times a day. Poppaea never travelled anywhere without a herd of female asses so she wouldn't run out.

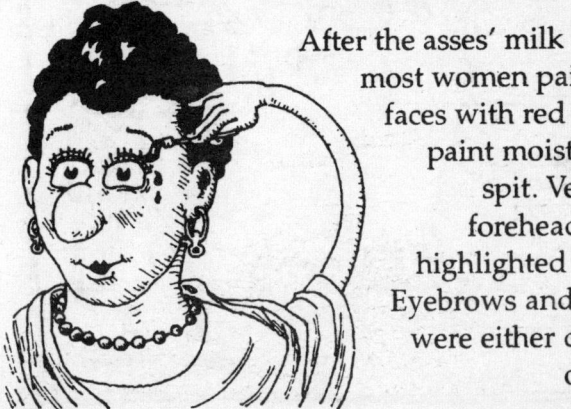

After the asses' milk treatment, most women painted their faces with red and white paint moistened with spit. Veins on the forehead might be highlighted with blue. Eyebrows and eyelashes were either dyed black or painted.

TUNICS AND TOGAS

Having bathed, done your hair and put on some make-up, the only thing left before leaving for dinner would be to get dressed, which in Roman times meant the two Ts - tunics or togas. Togas soon became fashionable among upper class Celts.

Togas were pieces of cloth about three times as long as the height of an average man and very difficult to wear. They were worn on smart formal occasions. At fifteen a boy would climb into a pure white *toga virilis*, the symbol of adulthood, and leave his youthful purple-fringed *toga praetextas* on the bedroom floor. Women also wore togas or a similar garment over their tunics, or *stolas*. At around fifteen girls also stepped out of their youthful purple-edged togas and were ready for marriage.

WAYS TO WEAR A TOGA
Part 1. (the only part there is)

WRONG
RIGHT

Tunics were comfortable everyday clothes, normally made of two pieces of cloth sewn up the sides and cut the same for both men and women.

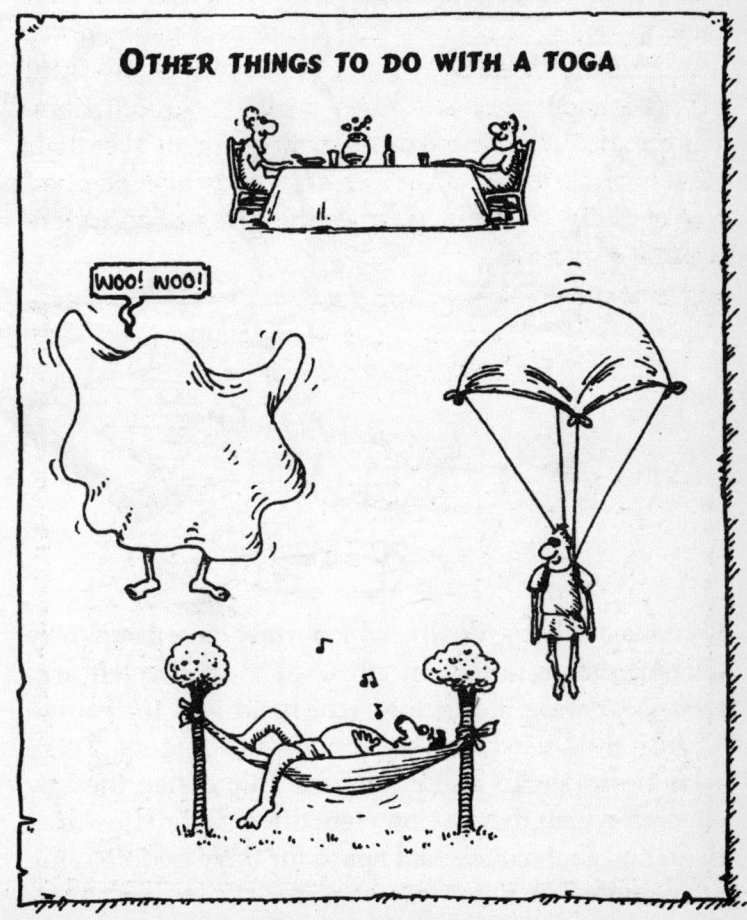

"I'M SO COMFY"
"SO AM I"

OTHER THINGS TO DO WITH A TOGA

"WOO! WOO!"

TAKE YOUR PLACE

Six was thought to be the ideal number for a small dinner party, although there was always space for nine, and obviously large banquets seated - or rather 'lay' - many more.

Romans ate lying down, which must have been very uncomfortable until you got used to it. The left arm took your weight and the right hand was for eating. Mainly they used knives, spoons and fingers. There were no forks. To make things a little easier, the low couches which they lay on were tilted slightly towards the table. Each couch had space for three people lying at an angle.

Dining-rooms were usually furnished with three couches arranged in a 'U' shape with a table in the middle. Slaves used the empty space in the middle for serving food.

TIME TO DINE

Poor people ate a simple diet of bread and other basic foods. But if possible nearly everyone spiced their food with *liquamen* which was the ketchup of the ancient world. Liquamen was basically rotten-fish-juice. It was salty, fishy, pale yellow and cheesy and Romans loved it.

RECIPE FOR LIQUAMEN

There were many different kinds of liquamen. Here's the recipe of the famous Roman gourmet Apicius:

1. Mix up some fish in a 'baking trough' with a lot of salt.

2. Leave overnight.

3. Cram into an earthenware container and leave open in the sun for up to three months, stirring from time to time.

4. Cover and store away. You can add some old wine at this stage.

5. Strain out the pale yellow residue and leave to mature.

MAD MORSELS

In Rome a normal meal might include fish, leeks, chick-peas, lupins and sausages, which are still cooked in roughly the same way in Italy today, two thousand years later. Nothing very exotic, apart from the lupins. The food in Britain would have been a bit different because of the northern climate. British oysters and mussels were very popular.

CAN'T EAT IT!

For a swanky banquet things became very elaborate. Details of many meals were written down. Which of these tasty trifles were not eaten by Romans? (Answers upside down):

potatoes

parrots' heads

tomatoes

camels' heels

ostrich heads

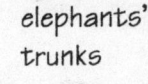

elephants' trunks

pearls

nightingales's brains

dormice sprinkled with honey and poppy seeds

Answers

Tomatoes and potatoes come from America which wouldn't be discovered until over a thousand years after the Romans had left Britain, but Romans ate pretty well anything else they could lay their hands on. Camels' heels were said to be a favourite of Queen Cleopatra, six hundred ostrich heads were served at one banquet given by the Emperor Heliogabalus, and the Emperor Caligula is said to have drunk pearls dissolved in vinegar.

What the Romans called *dormouse* was actually our field mouse. They were specially bred in hutches.

IT'S ENOUGH TO MAKE YOU SICK

Romans could eat a lot of food. The Emperor Vitellius once gave a banquet where two thousand costly fish and seven thousand birds were dished up. It was hard to eat so much food and some people had to make use of *vomitoria*, in other words they made themselves sick, often by tickling the back of the throat with a feather.

Many did this for health reasons since regular vomitings had been recommended by doctors since the time of the ancient Greek doctor, Hippocrates. But a lot of them did it just so they could eat some more. They 'vomited to eat, and ate to vomit,' as the writer Seneca put it.

GLADIATORS!

Leisure time the Roman way

> You can't eat dinner all day. With so much leisure time on our hands we Romans demanded other amusements.

Are you game for a game?

Romano-Britons liked to play, but 'games' were different then from how they are now. If a friend asks you to 'watch the game' with him or her, you probably assume that means a game of football. In Roman times it would probably have meant the spectacle of gladiators hacking each other to death.

> 'ERE WE GO, 'ERE WE GO, 'ERE WE GO, HERE WE GO, 'ERE WE GO-OH....

Roman games were put on either by the local council or by a rich citizen to show off his wealth. Entry was free, so staging games was a good way for a rich local politician to please the common people.

COLOSSAL OR WHAT? – THE COLOSSEUM

Games were staged in circuses and amphitheatres. Five amphitheatres have been found in Britain 👣. The rows for the seats were dug out of curving hill sides so that they looked down on the central stage area. They were used for all kinds of popular entertainment as well as 'games'.

> 1000 SAILORS WERE NEEDED TO WINCH OUT THE CANOPY (VELARIUM), USING 160 WINCHES

> 50,000 WAGON LOADS OF LIMESTONE WERE USED IN THE CONSTRUCTION, BROUGHT ALONG A SPECIALLY MADE ROAD FROM THE QUARRY

> 5 TONNE BLOCKS OF STONE AT THE BASE OF THE PILLARS

👣 At Dorchester, Silchester, Chichester, Cirencester and Carmarthen.

Compared to what was on offer in Rome, British amphitheatres were puny, pathetic and provincial. Rome had the *Colosseum*, which was absolutely massive. And in Rome the Emperor organized the games: he didn't want other wealthy men to get too popular.

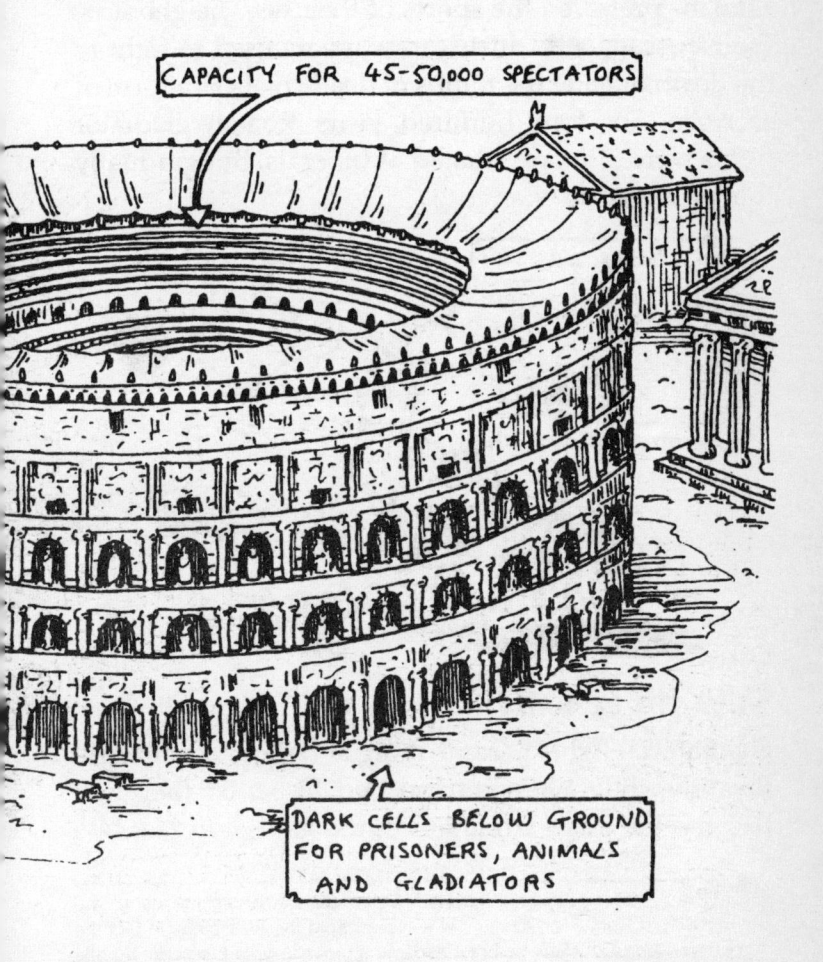

CAPACITY FOR 45-50,000 SPECTATORS

DARK CELLS BELOW GROUND FOR PRISONERS, ANIMALS AND GLADIATORS

TAME GAMES – AND NOT SO TAME

Early Roman games were based on Ancient Greek athletic competitions and included events such as the pentathlon. But athletics were too tame for Romans, who looked down on them. The famous doctor Galen said they made men 'idle, sleepy and slow-witted'.

Romans preferred the sports of their near neighbours, the Etruscans. Etruscan warriors used to fight to the death outside the tombs of dead chiefs as a form of sacrifice. For four hundred years Roman gladiator fights were also only staged at funerals. But gradually things started to change ...

GLAD. TO BE BAD

Gladiatorial fights became more and more popular. By the time the Colosseum opened in AD 80 they had become the main attraction in the games. In fact two

> The *Etruscans* ruled northern Italy before the Romans came along, and much of Roman civilization was copied from the Etruscans. In fact the three kings of Rome before it became a republic were Etruscan. No one has been able to decipher their writing. We know very little about them.

thousand people were killed in the Colosseum's arena within the first two weeks of the grand opening. Soon a constant supply of fresh fighters was needed to replace those who died.

There was never any shortage: gladiators were mostly either convicts, slaves or prisoners of war who had no choice but to fight. Few of them lived to old age; only a handful of fighters who won lots of fights were given the wooden sword of retirement and could live on as instructors.

The sport was so popular that some noblemen took it up (although it was always looked down on as an inferior occupation). There were even Emperors who played at being gladiators, which tended to be an unpleasant experience for the people they were fighting ...

HA! THAT'LL TEACH YOU!

Caligula fought an opponent who was armed with only a wooden sword - Caligula had a real one. Guess who won!

When the Emperor Commodus was in the ring with his bow and arrow, the people in the front rows were always nervous in case he decided to pick off a few spectators.

To provide variety for the audience, there were also women gladiators. Nero loved to watch them. They were eventually banned by the Emperor Septimus Severus in AD 200.

BAK TO SKOOL

Gladiators trained in special gladiator schools such as the one Spartacus escaped from at Capua. The gladiator school at Pompeii had seventy-one small sleeping rooms arranged in two stories around a practice hall. They practised with wooden swords and blunt weapons.

There were several types of gladiator:

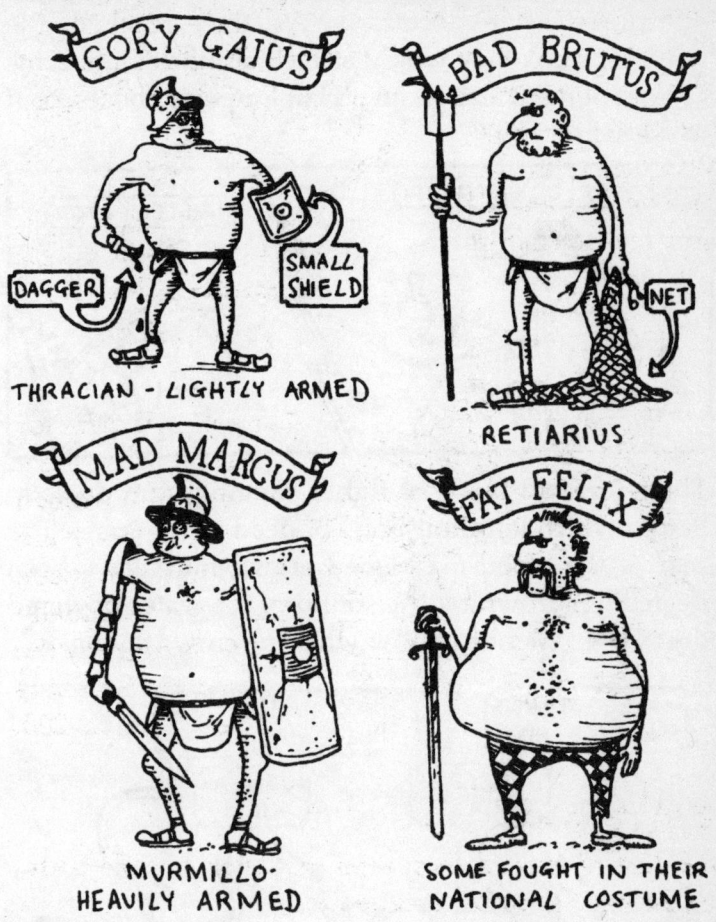

GORY GAIUS — DAGGER, SMALL SHIELD
THRACIAN - LIGHTLY ARMED

BAD BRUTUS — NET
RETIARIUS

MAD MARCUS
MURMILLO - HEAVILY ARMED

FAT FELIX
SOME FOUGHT IN THEIR NATIONAL COSTUME

GET ON WITH IT!

The evening before a fight the gladiators were given a special feast. Their loved ones came to say goodbye and the curious came to gawp at them while they ate. It was a sad occasion.

Next day they marched round the arena on the gleaming sand soon to be drenched in the blood of the slain, while around them the fifty thousand spectators murmured in expectation. As they reached the Emperor's box they would stretch out their right arms in front of them and shout: 'Hail Emperor, those about to die salute you!'.

There were all kinds of fights, ranging from duels to battles which left thousands of dead in the arena. The roar of the blood-maddened crowd must have been deafening, drowning the sound of the water-powered organ. We even know what the crowd shouted:

Romans liked organs. They were installed at arenas and race-tracks.

HOC HABET!

If defeated, a gladiator threw away his shield and raised a finger of his left hand as an appeal for mercy. The winner then decided whether or not to kill him, unless the Emperor was present, in which case the Emperor decided. The crowd helped with advice. Either they waved their handkerchiefs and put their thumbs up shouting: '*Mitte!*', meaning 'let him go', or they put their thumbs down and shouted: '*Iugula!*' meaning 'kill'. If the Emperor turned his thumb down the loser was killed immediately.

One slight reminder of ancient Etruscan customs remained. A man dressed as Charon, the Etruscan minister of fate, poked the dead with hot irons or struck him on the forehead with a hammer to make sure he was not faking. Finally slaves rushed on to the arena to shovel up the blood-soaked sand and sprinkle fresh sand before the next fight.

> The Ancient Greeks also believed in a figure called Charon, but he was different. The Greek Charon was an old man who ferried dead souls to the Greek paradise of Elysium.

ANIMAL MAGIC

The Romans loved animals - as entertainment. Some Emperors kept apes trained to drive chariots and sea-lions were taught to bark in answer to their names. There was even a group of four elephants trained to sit down to dinner and to carry a fifth in a litter.

WHO NEEDS STRAWS?

But what Romans liked best of all was watching animals being killed - or killing. It was almost better sport than the gladiators. The animals were shot and speared by specialists called *bestiarii*. Nine thousand animals were killed in the arena in the first hundred days after the Colosseum was opened.

Sometimes the animals were given a chance, as when naked spearman were matched against lions or leopards. At other times it was straightforward butchery, as when well-armed men speared harmless animals such as giraffes. And sometimes the animals had the advantage, as when unarmed Christians were pitted against lions by the Emperor Nero.

THE ANTICS OF ANDROCLES

Androcles was a Christian slave. He escaped from slavery and while he was on the run he hid in a cave. Unfortunately, or so it seemed, a lion entered the cave after him. But instead of gobbling him up, the lion held out its paw. Androcles saw that it was suffering from a large thorn embedded in its pad. He removed the thorn. The lion did not hurt him.

Later Androcles was recaptured and sentenced to fight a lion in the arena. Amazingly the lion which bounded towards him turned out to be the very same lion that he had helped previously.

Instead of attacking him the lion became all friendly and Androcles and the lion were allowed to live. Tradition has it that after the games were over, Androcles took his lion from inn to inn on a rope, collecting money.

MONEY FOR THE LION, MONEY FOR THE LION...

There was no limit to the slaughter of animals. From the farthest corners of the known world, wagon loads of captive creatures were trundled off to the Colosseum and the other amphitheatres of the Empire. No doubt a fair number found their way to Britain. Agents searched for rare and exotic creatures. In many regions, whole species were hunted out of existence. By the end of the Empire, there were no more lions in Mesopotamia, no more elephants in North Africa, no more tigers by the Caspian Sea.

CHARIOT FEVER

Gladiators were great, but the ultimate Roman sporting passion was chariot racing. It was almost a disease among them. There were four teams: Red, White, Blue and Green. People were fanatical about their teams, just as some people are fanatical about football teams today. One supporter of the Reds threw himself on the funeral pyre of his favourite jockey! Everyone from highest to lowest was involved. Nero had green sand sprinkled on the race track - guess which team he supported!

Fanatics would even sniff the dung of the horses to check that they were being well fed.

HMM, OATS WITH A PINCH OF BARLEY.

Modern football hooligans are bunny-rabbits compared to Roman chariot hooligans. In the Nika Riot of AD 532 in Constantinople between supporters of the Greens and the Blues, *30,000 people* are said to have died!

BLUES! GREENS!

COME TO THE CIRCUS

Chariot races were held in long oval race tracks called circuses. No remains of circuses have been found in Britain as yet, but it's hard to believe that the Romano-Britons didn't like chariot racing, given that the Celts had been such expert charioteers before the Romans came.

HUGE EGGS AND DOLPHINS WERE TAKEN DOWN ONE BY ONE TO COUNT THE NUMBER OF CIRCUITS.

GLISTENING SAND

Circus Maximus means 'Biggest Circus', and that's exactly what the Circus Maximus in Rome was - the biggest circus in the world. It could seat 150,000 spectators, some sitting on comfy cushions which they could buy at the entrance.

THE CENTRE WAS USED TO SHOW OFF PRISONERS OF WAR AND OTHER LOOT.

FAMOUS CHARIOTEERS WERE STARS.

EITHER TWO OR FOUR HORSES - USUALLY

REINS TIED AROUND WAIST

SLAVES ON DUTY AT THE CORNERS THREW BUCKETS OF WATER ON THE AXLES TO COOL THEM.

KNIFE TO CUT REINS IN AN ACCIDENT

NOTHING LASTS FOR EVER

We don't race chariots any more, and it's impossible to find a proper gladiator fight nowadays. All things come to an end.

In AD 402 a Christian monk called Telemachus tried to throw himself between two gladiators to stop them fighting. The official presiding over the games had him killed immediately. But when word of this reached the ear of the Emperor Honorius, he banned the games and they were never played again.

Chariot racing continued for a while longer. The last chariot race in Rome was run in an empty, ruined city in AD 549 in the presence of the barbarian invader, Totila the Goth.

ODD GODS

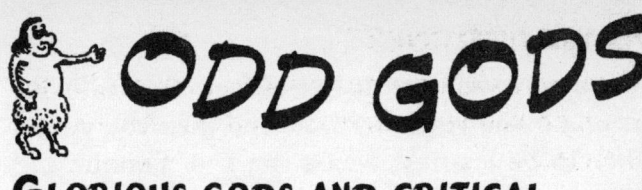

GLORIOUS GODS AND CRITICAL CHRISTIANS

SIX SPECIAL GODS

There were at least thirty thousand Roman gods. They ranged from the small and unusual to the grand and magnificent, such as Jove the greatest of all. Here are a few of the most important:

Jupiter, also called *Jove* or *Jupiter Optimus Maximus* - the 'Best and Greatest'

Juno - Jupiter's wife. Her sacred geese were kept in Rome. In 390 BC their clacking was said to have warned the Romans of an attack on their city by Celts.

Mars - god of war

Venus - goddess of love, fertility and female beauty

Apollo - god of light, reason and male beauty

Minerva - goddess of war and wisdom

As an example of an unusual sort of god, how about *Robigus* the god of red mildew?

WHAT'S THE DIFFERENCE?

Roman religion was very matter-of-fact. You said your prayers and made your sacrifices and then you got on with life. To be a priest was a mark of honour and good for your career. People were often given priesthoods in the way they are given knighthoods today.

Romans believed that everyone in the world worshipped the same basic gods, it's just that they called them by different names. This was a very convenient idea. Whatever country the Romans conquered they simply worked out what Roman god the local god was the same as, then worshipped both gods or one of them, whichever they chose. This meant that they never took offence at foreign religions, unless of course the foreign religion caused trouble like the Druids' did.

So the Celtic god *Belenus* was the same as the Roman god *Apollo*. It was just that in Rome Apollo had a splendid temple on the forum and in Britain he, or rather Belenus, was a spooky figure who kept a raven as his pet bird.

Similarly the mischievous, goat-horned, goat-legged

minor god *Pan* was the same as the horned Celtic god *Cernunnos*. And the Roman goddess of war and wisdom *Minerva* was the same as the Celtic goddess *Sul*. In fact the city of *Aquae Sulis* 🐾 (modern Bath) was often called *Aquae Sulis Minerva*.

A PACKET OF GODLETS

They also believed in a whole host of little gods. The little gods and demons would carry messages to the top gods if you asked them nicely 🐾 , perhaps with a little sacrifice. There was a whole host of demi-gods such as *centaurs* who were half man and half horse, and *satyrs* who had legs like goats. In every house there was a *lararium*, normally a cupboard in the form of a miniature temple. This was where the household gods, the *lares* and *penates* were kept.

Everything had its *genius*, or guardian spirit. There was a genius for every place and for every different group of people: every legion had its own genius.

🐾 Means 'Waters of Sul'.

🐾 Pre-Christian Romans could never understand why Christians thought Christianity was so different to other religions. After all, Christians believed in angels, which behaved pretty much like Roman demons.

107

That's why the Romans could come up with the mad idea of making their Emperors into gods: in a sense the Emperor, or at least his reign, already had a genius or spirit. So why not worship it?

Oh god!

Kings and emperors had been worshipped as gods in many civilizations before the time of the Romans, but it was Julius Caesar who started the fashion in Rome. He claimed 'divine honours' before he died. The first actual Roman emperor to be worshipped as a god was Augustus (63 BC - AD 14), although his godliness wasn't made official until after his death.

Soon the *Imperial Cult* as it was known became an important part of Roman rule. It was a good way of binding together all the different nations which made up the Empire. That's why almost as soon as they had conquered Britain the Romans built a massive temple to the Emperor Claudius at Colchester.

Eastern mysteries

Towards the end of the Empire several religions or cults from countries to the east became popular. The three most important were *Mithraism* from Persia, the worship of the Ancient Egyptian goddess *Isis*, and

Christianity which started in Palestine among followers of the Jewish religion.

MITHRAS

Temples dedicated to Mithras have been found all over the Empire including in London and on Hadrian's Wall. He was a spirit of pure light, and high moral standards were expected of his followers. They behaved a bit like Christians, holding sacred meals similar to Holy Communion as well as other secret rituals, although some of their rituals were rather different to the Christians' - for instance, having to lie under an iron grill while a bull was slaughtered on top of you.

ISIS

Isis was incredibly ancient, being one of the first Egyptian gods. She was a goddess of protection and healing. Her followers worshipped her in noisy ceremonies. She was very popular.

CHRIST

Christ was a Jew who had been crucified by the Romans. His followers believed in love and that Christ would return to Earth within a few years to save them and take them to heaven.

MAD MARTYRS

The Romans took a violent dislike to the Christians. The main problem was that, like the Jews, the Christians refused to recognize other people's gods.

Just imagine: you're a pagan, you've sown your fields

with coins so as to buy a good harvest from Ceres, the goddess of corn 🦶. Your neighbour is a Christian who not only doesn't sow his fields with coins, but goes out of his way to say that Ceres doesn't exist, thereby annoying Ceres, who then gets mad and stops the rain. It's enough to turn anyone off Christianity.

Romans devised a test to smoke out the Christians. Everyone was ordered to worship the Emperor. They had to pour some sacred oil then make a sacrifice and eat the meat. Anyone who refused could be executed. Many Christians refused, even when kind-hearted Roman officials pleaded with them, and offered to allow them to burn a little incense instead of making a sacrifice.

In several great waves of executions, Christians were fed to lions, burnt alive, crucified and disposed of in a hundred cruel ways. Their torture was the main attraction at many games.

To make matters worse, the Christians often welcomed their persecution. There were even volunteers! They firmly believed that whoever died for the faith, becoming a *martyr*, would go to heaven. They were so sure of this that very unchristian orgies took place in the cells beneath some North African arenas, among Christians waiting to be killed (after all they were going to go to heaven anyway): so much so that the local bishops had to write letters telling them to stop it.

🦶 This custom is why so many Roman coins are still found in our fields.

CONSTANTINE - A VERY IMPORTANT PERSON

Constantine's mother was the daughter of an innkeeper, but his father Constantius was a Caesar (a lesser position than emperor at that time). He took after his father and as soon as he was adult, he went after power like a bull terrier after a bone.

In AD 306 Constantius died at York after fighting in Scotland, beyond Hadrian's Wall. So it was at York that Constantine, who was one of his father's commanders, was declared Emperor by his father's army. He went on to defeat all his rivals and became a very powerful Roman Emperor. The reason he's so important is that he was the first Christian Emperor. It happened before his last great battle which was with a rival Emperor called Maxentius. Constantine saw a vision of a flaming cross in the sky. Because of this vision he believed that Christ helped him win the battle.

Constantine wasn't a Christian as most people might understand the word today; he murdered his wife and his son. But in AD 342 he made Christianity the state religion of the Empire - and changed the world.

Constantine is also famous for making ancient Byzantium, which he called *Constantinople* (modern Istanbul), the capital of the Eastern Roman Empire.

DO AS YOU HAVE BEEN DONE BY

After AD 342 Christianity swept through the Empire like a bush fire. Christians started popping up everywhere. After all, you now had to be a Christian to get a good job working for the Empire. The Christians lost no time in getting rid of the old Roman gods. It was Christians who destroyed the shrines and statues of the old religion.

Within a hundred years you could hardly find a follower of the old gods anywhere except in the deepest countryside. That's why followers of the old religion became known as *pagans*, from *paganus*, the Latin word for a country yokel or villager.

Nowadays pagan tends to mean an irreligious person - but perhaps Jupiter wouldn't have minded.

BEASTLY BARBARIANS

THE BEGINNING OF THE END

Like a cat with fleas, the Roman Empire was always scratching itself. Except they weren't fleas it was trying to get rid of, they were barbarians. And it wasn't scratching, it was fighting.

Apart from a short period in the second century AD, there was always trouble somewhere on the borders of the Empire. No matter how far the Romans advanced, there were always more barbarians beyond the border, barbarians who watched the Empire with greedy eyes. Many of them knew about Roman ways from first hand experience, perhaps having fought as auxiliaries. As the years passed, more and more barbarians were employed as soldiers by the Empire, for instance Saxon soldiers were stationed in Britain to fight off their fellow barbarians.

PICTING A FIGHT

Britain had its fair share of barbarian bust-ups. *Picts* raided across Hadrian's Wall, *Scots* (originally from Ireland) raided the west coast thus avoiding the Wall, and *Saxon* pirates plundered along the east coast as early as the third century. But as long as the Empire was strong it was easy to punish the trouble makers.

It didn't stay strong for ever ...

FOUR REASONS FOR WEAKNESS

1. Romans were never very good at choosing new emperors. More often than not, after one emperor died or was killed there was a civil war before a new emperor won power. They spent more time fighting each other than they did fighting barbarians.

2. Rich Romans behaved liked ostriches with their heads in the sand 🏇 They retreated to their luxurious villas in the country and spent less time and money on looking after the towns. They tried to pretend that things could go on as they were for ever.

3. Vast private estates called *latifundia* sprang up all over the Empire. The gap between rich and poor widened into a yawning chasm. Life at the bottom was tough, and to those at the bottom barbarian invasions must often have seemed like a way to escape oppression.

4. Some historians blame the rise of Christianity for the fall of Rome. Christianity was like a mole, burrowing away at the foundations of Roman rule such as Emperor worship and slavery.

Ostriches are said to bury their heads in the sand when in danger, believing that if they can't see the danger it doesn't exist.

COUNTDOWN TO COLLAPSE

5. By the 280s the North Sea was already crawling with Saxon pirates. A Celtic sailor called Carausius was ordered to clear them out. He seems to have been quite successful and several massive naval bases around the south and east coasts of England (the 'Forts of the Saxon Shore') may have been his work. But later he turned to piracy himself, declared himself Emperor and set up an independent empire in Britain for a while.

4. The first warning of more serious trouble came in 342 when the Emperor Constans, one of the sons of Constantine, had to make a hurried visit to Britain to repel barbarian raiders who had crossed over Hadrian's Wall. He beat them back.

3. By the 360s the barbarians were back. Picts, Scots, Attacotti 🐾 and Saxons attacked at the same time. Hadrian's Wall and the Forts of the Saxon Shore were overrun. Deserters from the army and escaped slaves joined the barbarians and roamed the land for two years, plundering and killing until order was restored.

2. In AD 409 most of the Roman army withdrew from Britain to fight in Europe. Realizing that their Roman governors had become more of a hindrance than a help, the Britons threw them out of the country and, as the historian Zosimus puts it: 'took up arms, braving danger for their independence and freed their cities of the barbarians ...'

🐾 The *Attacotti* were cannibals according to Saint Jerome. They came either from Ireland or the Western Isles.

1. By 410 the barbarians were back. The Britons appealed to the Emperor Honorius for help against the Saxons. He wrote back telling them he was unable to help them.

> Honorius' letter spelt the end of Roman rule in Britain, after nearly four hundred years. From then on the Romano-Britons had to fend for themselves as best they could.

FINIS

DARK AGES PAGES

Even after four hundred years of Roman rule, the Romano-Britons were still Celts beneath their togas. It seems that as they struggled to survive, they stopped behaving very much like Romans at all. There is evidence that in many places they retreated to their ancient hill-forts for safety. In fact one of the reasons that civilization died in Britain may well be that the ordinary British never cared as much for Roman ways as the Romans thought they did.

Even so, the next hundred and fifty years from AD 400-550 were a nightmare for the Romano-Britons, a nightmare from which they never woke up. They were battered by waves of barbarians from every direction, until at last they drowned in a sea of Saxon invaders and immigrants. Civilization had died in what is known as the *Dark Ages* 🐾.

🐾 'Dark' because there are very few written records from this time to shed light on what was happening.

If a Romano-Britain had returned from the grave a hundred and fifty years after Honorius wrote his letter, he would have had trouble recognizing his country. He would have seen that the villas, which had struggled on in the countryside until around AD 450 or even later were crumbling ruins, as were the great public buildings in the deserted towns (which some Saxons thought were the work of giants).

Perhaps the biggest shock would have been finding that most people spoke a different language. So many immigrants came from Germany that their language, Saxon, became the language of the country. Modern

English is based mainly on early Saxon. We speak the language of the barbarians, not of the defenders.

We speak a language which comes from the barbarians, but the majority of modern Britons are a mixture of both British and Saxon. It's strange to think that their ancestors were once involved in a savage war with each other.

But that's history for you.

Finis

Although based on Saxon, modern English contains many words taken from Latin at a later date, mostly via French which is based on Latin.

Finis is Latin for 'The End'.

ROMAN RELICS

COULD *YOU* BE A ROMAN? (PART 4)

The Romans really were like giants. Their influence is everywhere - in our language, our laws, our arts and our buildings, even in the weeds in our gardens. It would take several books the size of this one to list a fraction of what we have inherited from them. So which one of the following have we *not* inherited from the Romans?

a   rabbits
b   beer
c   towns ending in ester, cester and chester etc.
d   nettles
e   Saturday
f   French, Spanish, Romanian and Italian languages
g   words ending in 'ion'
h   the months of the year
i   lots of straight roads such as the A5

Saturday was named after the god Saturn

Romans are said to have whipped themselves with nettles for warmth

COULD *YOU* BE A ROMAN? - ANSWERS

Score 10 points for each right answer

Part 1	Part 2	Part 3	Part 4
1 b	a 23	c	beer
2 a	b 47		
3 c	c 174		

Less than 30   Useless - go back to barbarism
        30+   Not bad - time to take out the toga
        60+   First class - lie down for dinner

INDEX

Africa 8, 100
Agricola, Emperor 37
Amphitheatres 62, 67, 89, 90-7
Ancient British tribes 12
Ancient Britons 5, 11-16, 18, 35, 60
Ancient Greeks 13, 79, 92, 97
Androcles 99
Anencletus 52
Anglesey 36, 37, 38
Antonine Wall 42
Antoninus Pius, Emperor 42
Aqueducts 9, 62
Aquilifer 29
Armour 16, 25
Army, Roman 24-33
Asses' milk 81
Attacotti 117
Augustus 46
Aulus Plautius 10, 22, 18

Ballista 28
Banquets 77, 84, 85,
Barbarians 113-118
Basilicas 66
Baths 66, 78
Bestiarii 98
Boudicca 27, 37-9
Brigantes 20
Byzantine Empire 8

Caesar's Invasion of Britain 10, 11
Calendar 46, 47
Caligula, Emperor 7, 21, 49, 93
Camps 32, 33
Camulodunum 19, 35, 38, 63, 108
Canterbury 64
Capua 54, 94
Caracalla, Emperor 60
Caratacus 19, 20, 23
Carausius 116
Cartimandua 20
Catapults 28
Centuries 28
Centurions 29, 30
Chariots 18, 20, 100-4
Charon 97
Children 73-6
Christians 62, 107, 109-12, 115
Christmas 57
Cicero 57
Circuses 62, 102-103
Circus Maximus 103
Citizens 59, 60, 52
Claudian Invasion of Britain 6, 7, 18, 19
Claudius, Emperor 6, 7, 10, 11, 21, 22, 23, 60
Cleopatra 48, 81
Cohorts 28
Colonies 63, 64
Colosseum 90-3
Commodus, Emperor 94
Consentius 65
Constans, Emperor 116

123

Constantine, Emperor 111
Constantinople 101, 111
Consuls 46
Crassus 54
Crucifixion 54
Cunobelin 19

Decimation 30
Delos 53
Discipline (Roman army) 30
Dolphins 102
Domitian, Emperor 71
Druids 11, 36, 37, 75, 106

Egypt 48
Elephants 10, 98
Elysium 97
Entrails 14
Etruscans 92, 97

Face masks 80, 81
Food 85-7
Forum 66
Fosse Way 40
Freedmen 45, 57-8

Gallienus, Emperor 80
Games 89, 90-2
Gladiators 54, 89-99
Gladiator schools 94
Gods, 35, 57, 66, 105-9

Hadrian's Wall 42, 43, 111, 114, 116-7
Hair 5, 15, 16, 17, 60, 80
Hair dye 15
Hastati 25
Head-hunting 14
Hill-forts 12
Hippocrates 88

Holidays 52, 57
Honorius, Emperor 104, 118, 120
Hypocaust 71

Iceni 37
Imperial cult 108
Imperial messengers 42
Insulae 68
Isis 108-9

Jesus Christ 54
Julius Caesar 10, 11, 46-8, 64

Knights 45, 50

Latifundia 115
Laws 58-9
Legatus 29
Legions 28-9, 31
Liquamen 85, 86
London 38, 40, 52, 64

Make-up 80-1
Marc Antony 48
Marius' mules 31
Marriage 72, 73, 76
Martyrs 109, 110
Maxentius, Emperor 111
Mile Fort 42
Mirmilliones 95
Mistletoe 36
Mithraism 108-9
Mosaics 70

Nero, Emperor 51, 62, 80, 94, 98, 101
Nika riot 101
Nomenclatores 55

Octavius, Emperor 46-8, 108
Officers 29
Ostriches 115

Pagans 112
Paterfamilias 58-59
Patricians 50, 67
Peculium 58
Pedagogues 74
Pentathalon 92
Persian Empire 9
Picts 114, 117
Plebeians 50
Pliny 22
Poison 39, 48
Pompey 48
Poppaea 80-1
Poppaeana 80
Praetorian Gaurd 49
Prasutagus 38
Princeps 25
Procurator 50

Religion 106-10
Retiarii 95
Rhetors 76
Roads 39-42
Roman Empire 7-9
Rome 62-3

Saint Jerome 117
Saint Paul 60
Saturnalia 57
Saxons 114, 116, 117, 118, 119, 120, 121
School 74, 75, 76
Scots 114, 117
Seneca 56, 88
Septimus Severus, Emperor 79, 94

Slaves 21-2, 41, 45, 52-8, 68, 74, 97, 103
Soap 78
Spartacus 54, 94
Stola 17
Strigils 78
Suetonius Paulinus 37, 40
Swords 26, 27, 93

Tacitus 36
Tax 50
Telemachus 104
Temples 23, 35, 66
Tepidarium 78
Tessarius 30
Thracians 95
Togas 17, 64, 82
Togodumnus 19
Toilets 66, 68
Totila the Goth 104
Toys 74
Traffic jams 62, 63
Triarii 25
Tribunes 29, 50
Triumphs 21, 22, 23
Tunics 82, 83

Velites 25
Veterans 63
Villas 67-9, 70-1, 115, 120
Vitellius, Emperor 88
Vomiting 88

Water organs 96
Watling Street 39-40
Wicker men 36

Zosimus 117

Now Read On

If you want to know more about the Romans in Britain, see if your local library or bookshop has any of these books.

THE ROMAN WORLD
By Mike Corbishley (Kingfisher History Library 1986). The first part of this book gives you the entire history of Rome from its foundation by two twins who were suckled by a wolf right up to its last days under the barbarians. And the second half has got enough information to paralyse a professor!

HOW WOULD YOU SURVIVE AS AN ANCIENT ROMAN?
By Anita Ganeri (Watts Books 1994). A beautifully illustrated book which gives you the low-down on all aspects of life among the Romans.

EVERYDAY LIFE IN ROMAN AND ANGLO-SAXON TIMES
By Marjorie and CHB Quennell (Batsford Ltd. 1959) There's loads of information about the Romans in the first half of this book. It was written some time ago but it's still one of the best reads around. Be careful you don't get information indigestion!

ANCIENT ROME
By Simon James (Dorling Kindersley 1990, Eyewitness Guides series). This book is packed with wonderful photographs of actual objects used by Romans as they went about their lives. So next time you come across something Roman you'll be sure to know what it is!

What they don't tell you about

ANGLO-SAXONS

By Bob Fowke

Dedicated to *Trimilchi*, the saxon month when cows were milked three times a day.

A division of Hodder Headline Limited

> Hallo, my name's Ethelfrithelfroth, and if you can say that you can say anything. I'm a Saxon woman and I'm tough as a leather garter. Come with me and I'll show you all about the Anglo-Saxons. I hope you're tough too: this book is not for the faint-hearted ...

What They Don't Tell You About Anglo-Saxons first published as a single volume in Great Britain in 1998 by Hodder Children's Books.

Text and illustrations copyright © Bob Fowke 1998

CONTENTS

SAXFAX
BEFORE WE BEGIN
Page 5

ROMAN REMAINS
BRITAIN BEFORE THE ROMANS
Page 14

SAX ATTAX!
WE'VE COME TO STAY
Page 18

CELTIC COUNTERATTAX!
THE BRITISH FIGHT BACK
Page 28

CRAZY KINGDOMS
KINGS AND THEIR COMPANIONS
Page 35

FIVE PENCE PER FINGER!
PAW LAWS ...
Page 46

DOWN ON THE FARM
LIFE IN THE MUD
Page 55

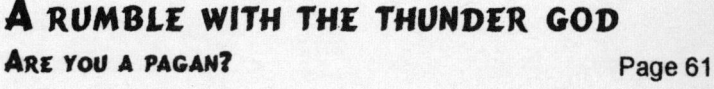

A RUMBLE WITH THE THUNDER GOD
ARE YOU A PAGAN?
Page 61

Watch out for the *Sign of the Foot*! Whenever you see this sign in the book it means there are some more details at the *FOOT* of the page. Like here.

ANGELS AND DEVILS
TAMING THE PAGANS
Page 69

BRITISH BELIEVERS
... AND THEIR MONKEY BUSINESS
Page 77

WISE WOMEN
AND MAD MISSIONARIES
Page 87

STRIKING VIKINGS
OH NO! THE BARBARIANS ARE BACK!
Page 95

OUR ALFRED
EVERYONE NEEDS A HERO
Page 103

SAXONS STUFFED!
ALL GOOD THINGS COME TO AN END
Page 110

ARE YOU AN ANGLE OR A SAXON?
- OR A NORMAN OR A CELT?
Page 118

INDEX	Page 122
NOW READ ON	Page 126
ABOUT THE AUTHOR	Page 127

SAXFAX

BEFORE WE BEGIN

A SAXON FEAST

UGGHFF!
SPLOOOSH!
SPILLED MEAD

There's a feast in the mead hall 🐾. It's been going on for months, although that's nothing special if you're a Saxon warrior. And it's been great - there's been boasting and drinking for breakfast, followed by drinking and boasting with a spot of poetry for lunch, and in the evenings there's been lots more drinking - and more boasting! After all, what's a warrior to do with his spare time?

All right, so there's been the odd fight. These lads have been feasting too long. It's time to head out on a proper war party ...

🐾 Mead is an alcoholic drink made from honey.

WHERE WILD WARRIORS WANDER

The Saxons were wild warriors from northern Europe who conquered what is now England in the years between AD 450 and 700. Early Saxons couldn't read or write so they didn't leave us any written records. We know very little about them - but we do know that fighting was what they liked doing best.

These wild warriors belonged to several barbarian nations or tribes and their homeland was in the area now covered by northern Holland and Germany, far beyond the reach of the civilized Roman Empire at that time. They're called *Anglo-Saxons* because their two largest nations were the Angles and the Saxons, but they're often just called *Saxons* for short.

AD stands for *Anno Domini*, or 'Year of Our Lord', and means the number of years after the birth of Christ. This system of dating was introduced into Britain by the Anglo-Saxons.

Barbarian was a word used by the Romans to described uncivilized tribes. It comes from the Greek word for a foreigner.

The Anglo-Saxons believed that they were descended from a hero called *Sceaf* who had been washed up on a northern beach in an open boat in the dim and distant past. Boats were important to the Saxons. They lived near the sea and were expert sailors. In fact, there had been Saxon pirates in the North Sea for hundreds of years before they conquered Britain, so much so that the name *Saxon* was used as another word for 'pirate' among the poor old Romans who first suffered their attacks.

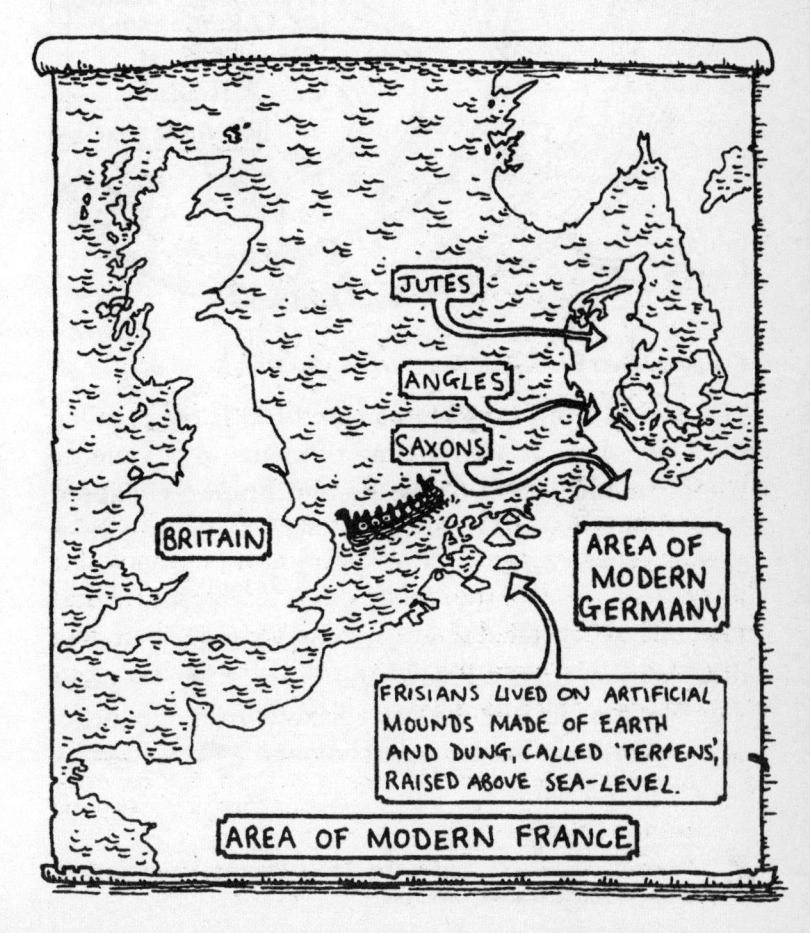

JUTES
ANGLES
SAXONS
BRITAIN
AREA OF MODERN GERMANY
FRISIANS LIVED ON ARTIFICIAL MOUNDS MADE OF EARTH AND DUNG, CALLED 'TERPENS', RAISED ABOVE SEA-LEVEL.
AREA OF MODERN FRANCE

Year beer

Saxons often drank from *drinking horns*.

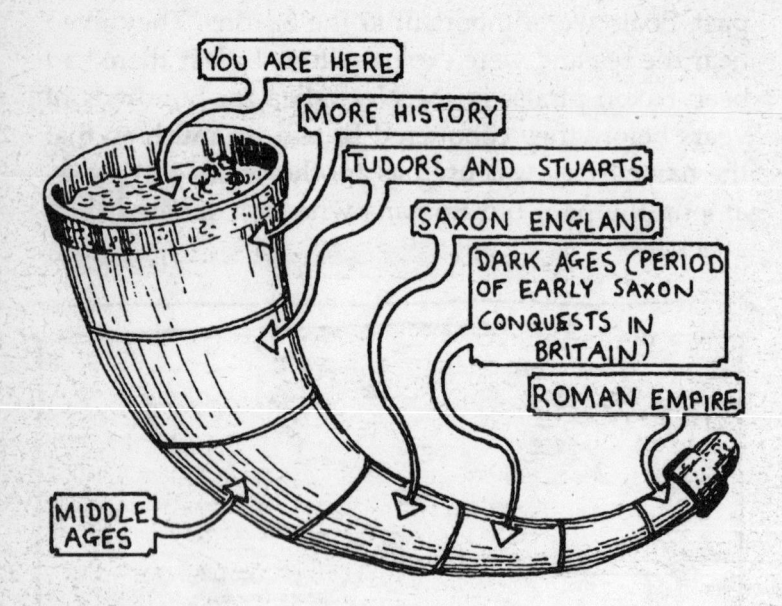

- YOU ARE HERE
- MORE HISTORY
- TUDORS AND STUARTS
- SAXON ENGLAND
- DARK AGES (PERIOD OF EARLY SAXON CONQUESTS IN BRITAIN)
- ROMAN EMPIRE
- MIDDLE AGES

Black out!

The period from AD 400 to around 600 is often called the *Dark Ages*. It was a time of chaos and violence when the old world of the Roman Empire collapsed beneath a thousand barbarian attacks, including those of the early Saxons.

They're called the 'Dark Ages' because we know so little about them. Historians have had to piece together the story of the early Saxons from a handful of clues, mostly battered parchments written by their angry enemies.

Paper was unknown in Europe at that time. Everything was written on a sort of leather, called parchment.

CLUES IN THE DARKNESS

Triads (no, not Chinese gangsters!) are very early Welsh or British poems.

Gildas was a British monk who wrote the *'Story of the Loss of Britain'* in AD 547.

Nennius, another British monk, wrote about Saxon attacks.

Saxon kings made *king lists* of their royal ancestors. Later these lists were written down.

The *Venerable Bede* was a Saxon monk who wrote a history of his people around AD 730.

The *Anglo-Saxon Chronicle* was started around AD 890 but refers back to earlier times.

Beowulf is a poem about Saxon heroes around the time of their conquest of Britain (see page 43).

MR AND MRS SAXON

The Roman writer Tacitus says the early Germans were large people with blue eyes and reddish or fair hair. This is probably what most of the early Anglo-Saxons looked like.

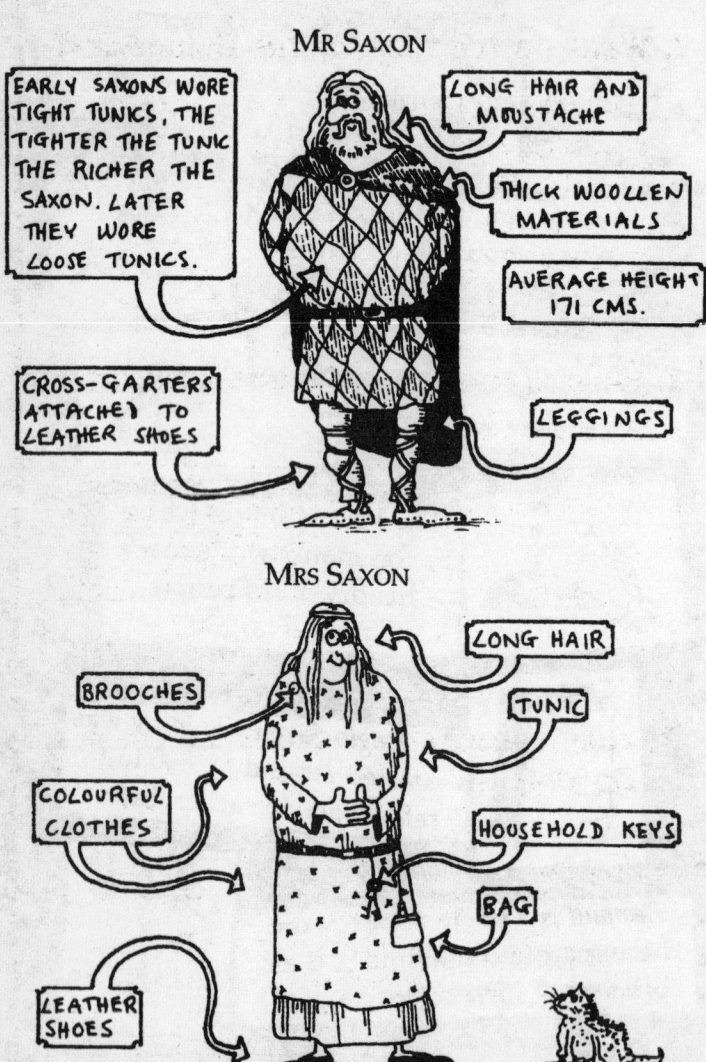

MR SAXON

- EARLY SAXONS WORE TIGHT TUNICS, THE TIGHTER THE TUNIC THE RICHER THE SAXON. LATER THEY WORE LOOSE TUNICS.
- LONG HAIR AND MOUSTACHE
- THICK WOOLLEN MATERIALS
- AVERAGE HEIGHT 171 CMS.
- CROSS-GARTERS ATTACHED TO LEATHER SHOES
- LEGGINGS

MRS SAXON

- LONG HAIR
- BROOCHES
- TUNIC
- COLOURFUL CLOTHES
- HOUSEHOLD KEYS
- BAG
- LEATHER SHOES

ARE YOU IGNORANT?

Check it out - are you the right type to be a seriously savage Saxon?
Part 1

1. WHAT DO YOU THINK OF THE DARK AGES?

a. Lovely time to be alive. Wish they could go on for ever
b. Horrible, why doesn't someone invent the electric light
c. Dark Ages? What's that?

2. WHAT IS THE ANGLO-SAXON CHRONICLE?

a. A costume drama series on television
b. A Saxon newspaper of the period
c. A record of events during the Saxon period

3. YOUR FRIEND STARTS RECITING A POEM. DO YOU?...

a. Tell him or her to shut up and stop being so sissy
b. Sit back and enjoy it
c. Listen and then tell him or her that you could do better

Answers on page 121

THE GOOD, THE BAD AND THE BARBARIC

The early Saxons were barbarians whose idea of a quiet night in was a drunken bone-fight in the mead hall. But over time the Saxons settled down and many later Saxons were saints and statesmen who helped to re-civilize Europe and end the barbaric Dark Ages.

Between them, the bad early Saxons and the good later Saxons made a huge impact on Britain. In AD 449, when the Saxons first arrived in force, people in Britain spoke a bit of Latin, and *Brythonic*, a language like Welsh. Two hundred years later most people in what is now *England* spoke an early form of *English*. They obeyed *English* laws and lived in *English* towns and villages.

You see, the early Saxons came as warriors, but they stayed on as settlers. As the years went by they either mingled with the locals or drove them out. The Angles were the largest group of settlers, so nearly everyone in what is now England came to call themselves Angles or *Aenglisc* which is where the words *English* and *England* come from.

> Lots of Saxon names start with 'ae'. The two letters together are pronounced a bit like the 'a' in 'add'. So Aenglisc is pronounced 'Anglisc'.

ROMAN REMAINS

BRITAIN BEFORE THE SAXONS

Britain at the time of the Saxon invasions was full of British people, believe it or not. The British were Celts and the language they spoke, Brythonic, was a Celtic language, whereas the Saxons were Germans and Saxon was a German language.

THE STORY SO FAR

AD 43 The Romans invade Britain. The British Celts fight back bravely, but their war-chariots are no match for the Roman armies. The British living in the area of modern England and Wales are defeated and all of Britain, except Scotland, becomes a province of the Roman Empire.

AD 43-280 The British become civilized members of the Roman Empire. They have roads and cities. The rich live in comfortable houses, and most people learn to speak Latin, the Roman language, as well as Brythonic. They are often called Romano-Britons.

Celts, or Celtic speaking people, once lived in much of northern and western Europe. Those that lived in England were mainly tall with fair hair. Those in Wales, Ireland and Scotland were mainly smaller with dark hair.

AD 280 Saxon pirate attacks cause serious problems. The Romans build a number of massive forts along the coast, known as the *Forts of the Saxon Shore*.

AD 360 The first collapse: barbaric Picts from Scotland, Scots from Ireland and Saxons overrun Britain. Chaos reigns for two years.

AD 409 The Roman army is withdrawn from Britain to fight other barbarians on mainland Europe. The British must defend themselves against barbarian attack.

AD 449 Saxon warriors, who have been invited into Britain to help defend the Romano-British against the Scots, turn on their British guests - the Saxon conquests have begun.

The word *Pict* comes from the Latin for 'painted'. They were northern Celts and probably decorated themselves with a blue dye called woad.

The *Scots* came from Ireland originally. Until around AD 1400 the word 'Scot' meant an Irishman.

SOFT CITIES

How would you feel if your town was attacked by a pack of barbarians armed with swords and spears? Pretty upset probably. That's how the Britons must have felt in AD 450. For four hundred years Britain had been ruled by Rome. They had cities, roads, town halls, public baths and libraries, and they even had central heating. They were civilized. They didn't want to be bothered with war and fighting - but Saxons did!

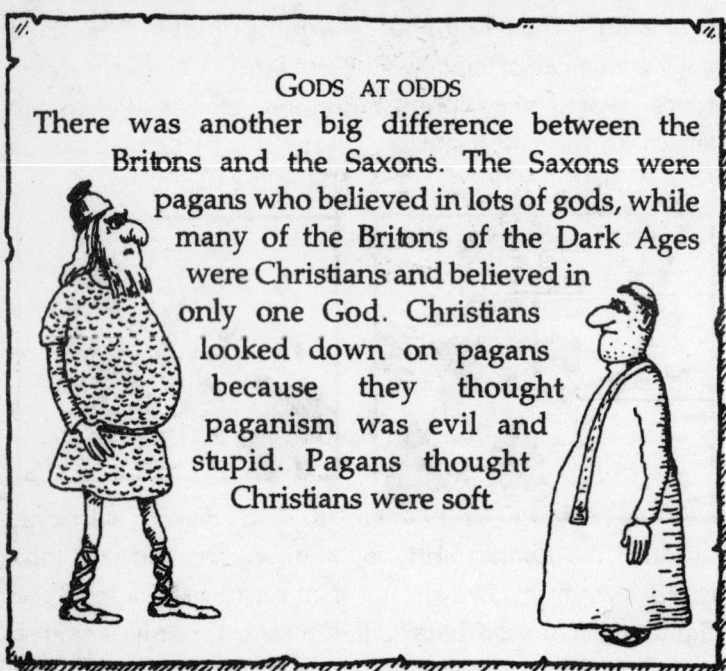

GODS AT ODDS

There was another big difference between the Britons and the Saxons. The Saxons were pagans who believed in lots of gods, while many of the Britons of the Dark Ages were Christians and believed in only one God. Christians looked down on pagans because they thought paganism was evil and stupid. Pagans thought Christians were soft.

SWORDS FOR SALE

Saxons and other barbarians liked fighting. They also liked money. So, for hundreds of years the Romans paid barbarians to fight *for* them instead of *against* them. On the borders of the Roman Empire there were often Saxon soldiers fighting alongside the regular

Roman army. Saxons like this were probably living in Yorkshire before AD 400. It worked fine as long as the Romans were strong enough to control them - but what would happen if the Saxons turned against their employers?

In AD 449 the Britons were about to find out ...

SAX ATTAX!

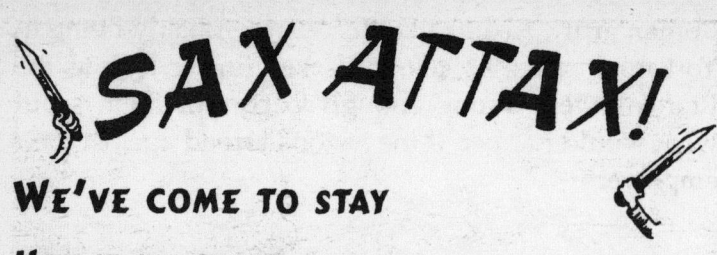

WE'VE COME TO STAY

HOW IT ALL BEGAN

The Roman province of Britain was alone like a lost duckling without its mother duck after the Roman army left Britain around AD 409. The Romano-Britons struggled on alone, but all kinds of barbarians hovered greedily beyond the borders, ready to pounce.

Forty years later barbarian attacks were getting out of hand. It seems that a British leader named Vortigern, the 'Proud Tyrant', asked a band of Saxon warriors to fight for him against the barbarian Scots. These Saxon warriors came in three or more ships and landed at a place called *Ypines Fleot* in Kent 🐾. Their leaders were two tough killers called Hengist and Horsa. Many more warriors soon joined them.

The name of the county of Kent comes from the British tribe which used to live there, the Cantii.

Just six years after they arrived, Hengist and Horsa quarrelled with Vortigern, perhaps because he hadn't paid them. There was a battle, the first of many such battles. Horsa was killed but the Saxons won. Then in 457, at a place called *Crecgan Ford*, also somewhere in Kent, four thousand Britons were killed. The remainder of the British army fled before the Saxons 'like fire' until they reached the safety of London. The first Saxon kingdom in Britain had been born.

Other Saxon chiefs were quick to follow the example of Hengist and Horsa. In 477 the founders of the kingdom of the South Saxons, or Sussex as we call it today, landed in three ships, killed many Britons and drove others into a wood near the Roman fort of Anderida - modern Pevensey. In 491 the Saxons besieged the fort itself and killed all the Britons inside it. The Britons were battered by Saxon attacks all along the south and east coasts.

LET'S GO BOATING

Saxon ships were large open rowing boats. About thirty warriors manned the oars and a typical war party was made up of three boats and about a hundred men 🐾 As well as riding the ocean waves, they could be rowed in shallow waters, ideal for inland attacks up rivers or for landing on deserted beaches late at night.

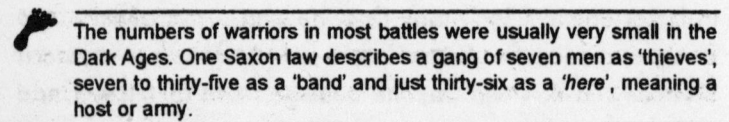

WE'RE COMING TO GET YOU

TARRED OVERLAPPING PLANKS

NO SAIL

ABOUT TWENTY-FOUR METRES LONG

NO KEEL

🐾 The numbers of warriors in most battles were usually very small in the Dark Ages. One Saxon law describes a gang of seven men as 'thieves', seven to thirty-five as a 'band' and just thirty-six as a *'here'*, meaning a host or army.

🐾 The keel is a plank which juts down beneath the ship to stop it rolling from side to side.

WHAT A BOAR!

The warriors who scrambled to shore from their shallow boats were well armed.

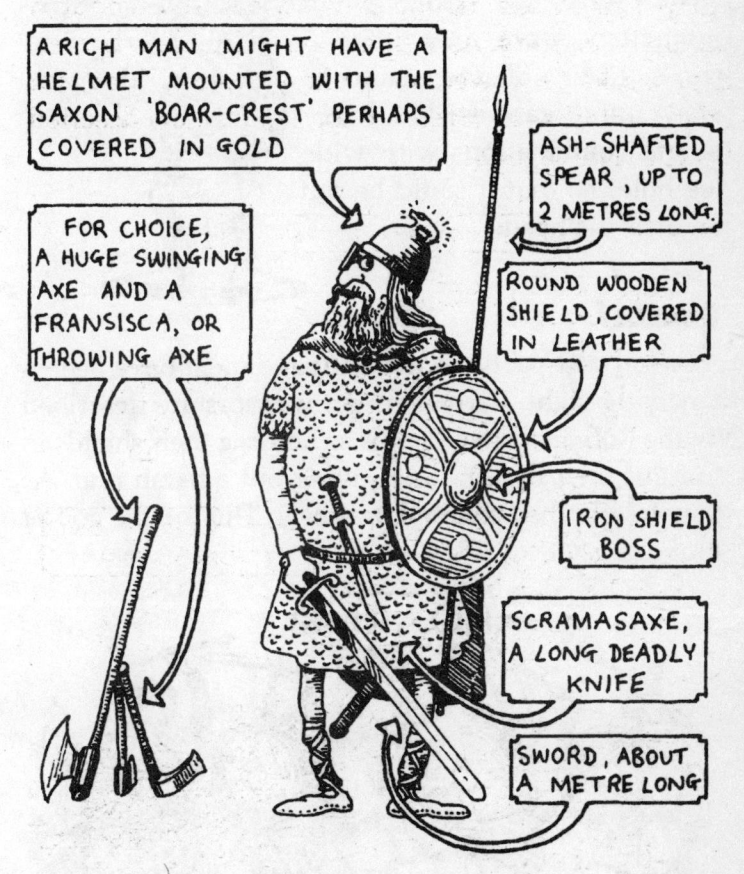

A RICH MAN MIGHT HAVE A HELMET MOUNTED WITH THE SAXON 'BOAR-CREST' PERHAPS COVERED IN GOLD

ASH-SHAFTED SPEAR, UP TO 2 METRES LONG.

FOR CHOICE, A HUGE SWINGING AXE AND A FRANSISCA, OR THROWING AXE

ROUND WOODEN SHIELD, COVERED IN LEATHER

IRON SHIELD BOSS

SCRAMASAXE, A LONG DEADLY KNIFE

SWORD, ABOUT A METRE LONG

Swords were very precious. Ordinary warriors couldn't afford them. They were handed down from one generation to the next and carefully looked after. In the tenth century, the Saxon Prince Athelstan gave a sword to his brother which had been owned three hundred years earlier by a famous king called Offa (more on him on page 105).

Early German warriors fought naked or wearing only short cloaks, but by Saxon times the rich noblemen wore iron mail shirts. Later still the mail was sewn into a garment like knee-length combinations with wide leg holes so that it could be put on over the head.

CHARGE!

A Saxon war-party on the rampage must have been a terrifying sight. Early German warriors are described by the Roman writer Tacitus as holding their shields in front of their mouths and giving out a harsh roar. As they fought they chanted praises to Thunor, the god of thunder.

Battles tended to be a scrum of fights between individual soldiers. Expert warriors were respected in the same way as famous sportsmen are today. Here's a later description of a fight of one against two, from

'The Lives of the Two Offas' written in St Albans. Two men have attacked the handsome young Offa:

> *With one stroke of his sword he struck down one of them, slashing off the crest of his helmet and piercing the skull to the brain, and casting him down as the death-rattle sounded. Then he rapidly pursued the other ... prostrating him with a lethal wound.*

During the battle the warriors might plant a standard in the ground. On the tip of the standard would be the figure of a fierce animal, often a boar or a stag. Around the standard they might form the Saxon *scildburgh* or 'shield wall'. To make a shield wall the warriors formed a line or a circle with their shields touching each other and awaited the advance of their enemies.

The early Saxons showed no mercy to their victims. Women and children were often slaughtered during their raids. Later the British monk Adomnan suggested a 'Law of the Innocents' to protect women and children. British kings accepted this law - but the Saxons didn't.

The British and the Saxons disagreed about a lot of things.

23

SOLDIER, SOLDIER

Check it out - are you the right type to be a seriously savage Saxon?
Part 2

1. IT'S YOUR BIRTHDAY. WHICH PRESENT WOULD YOU LIKE BEST?

a. A sword
b. A huge swinging axe
c. A toy soldier called Egfrith

2. SOMEONE HAS CHALLENGED YOU TO A FIGHT IN THE PLAYGROUND. DO YOU?..

a. Go home early complaining of a headache
b. Silently prepare for battle
c. Charge at him or her with a harsh roar

3. WHAT IS A SHIELD BOSS?

a. The leader of a war party
b. The iron centre of a shield
c. The metal rim of a shield

Answers on page 121

WHAT IS THE MEANING OF BIRMINGHAM?

If all the Saxons had been warriors they would not have changed the world as much as they did. But they weren't. Thousands upon thousands of Saxon settlers followed the warriors. They changed the face of Britain for good. We know where many of them settled from place names. Does where you live end in 'ton, 'ham, or 'ing?

Ingas meant a group of followers. So *Haestingas*, or *Hastings* as we call it today, is where the family and followers of *Haesta* settled. Likewise *Reading* is where the followers of *Reada* started to farm.

Tun meant a village, so if your village ends in 'ton as in *Drayton*, you too live in an early Saxon settlement.

Ham meant home. Places ending in 'ham such as *Swaffham* were also started by the Saxons.

Now you can work out the meaning of *Birmingham*!

Birmingham means 'Beornmund's people's home'. The Beornmund bit was shortened to 'Birm'. Wonder what Birm would have made of that?

MIXED MESSAGES

The Saxons were ruthless warriors, but it's wrong to think that they drove all the British out of England. More likely, a lot of British people stayed on under their new rulers. Many would have had no choice, having been enslaved. The Saxon word for the British, *wahl* or *welisc* meaning 'foreigner', was also used to mean a slave.

But it wasn't all fighting. There must have been a lot of mixing between the two cultures. To start with, it seems that the Saxons often settled on unfarmed land between the old Roman villa estates, which were probably still being farmed by the British. In other places British and Saxon farmers lived side by side in the same villages.

Very early on it seems that there were marriages between Saxon and British men and women. For instance, *Cerdic*, the war chief who founded Wessex, the Kingdom of the West Saxons, was first in the line

---

Welisc is where the word *Welsh* comes from. The British didn't call themselves Welsh. They called themselves the *Cymry*, meaning 'companions'.

of kings from which all later English kings are descended. His name is Celtic so he probably had a British mother. Likewise one of the earliest kings of Lindsey, a Saxon kingdom in Lincolnshire, was called Caedbad which is based on the Celtic word *cad* meaning a battle.

We know that Saxons and British Celts living in England both tended to be large with fair hair. Within a few generations, once they were all speaking English, it was impossible to tell one from the other.

CELTIC COUNTERATTAX!

THE BRITISH FIGHT BACK
BUT FIRST - THE SAXONS SPREAD OUT

> There was a lot more fighting than mixing to begin with. In the fifty years from 450-500 many Saxon armies savagely attacked lands controlled by the British.

AD 495 Cerdic, founder of Wessex, the kingdom of the West Saxons, lands near Southampton with five ships. In a few years he conquers a large kingdom in the south of England.

By AD 500 Angles have landed in the east of Britain, founding the kingdom which will become known as East Anglia and making their way north of London into the southern Midlands.

By AD 500 Saxon pirates set up pirate bases along the north east coast. Later this region will become Northumbria, one of the most powerful Saxon kingdoms.

By AD 500 many Britons have fled across the English Channel. They form a new kingdom in what is now the French region of *Brittany*.

BRITISH BLOBS

When the Roman bishop Germanus visited Kent in 447, the leaders of the British still dressed like Roman nobles. They were *'brilliant in dress and surrounded by a fawning multitude'*. Just fifty years later Roman civilization had all but disappeared under pressure from Saxon attacks. The British kingdoms were ruled by warrior kings who behaved very like Saxon kings.

It was tough for the Britons. Their old Romano-British civilized way of life was under threat from all sides. But odd blobs of civilized Romano-British life lingered on in parts of Britain.

- The Roman fountains kept on flowing in Carlisle until at least 670.

- There was still a small British kingdom called Elmet in Yorkshire around 620.

- But the main British blobs were on the edges of England:

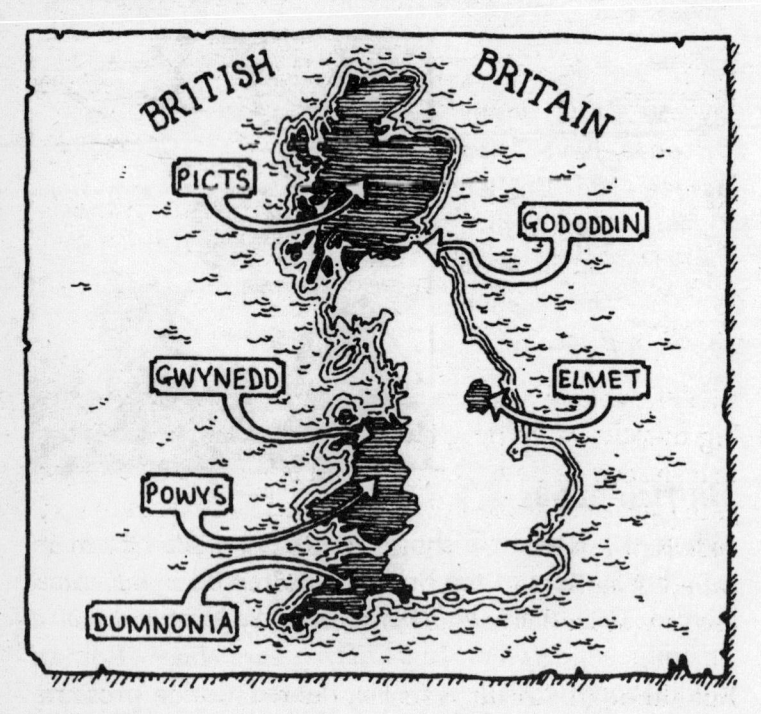

BRITISH BRITAIN

PICTS • GODODDIN • GWYNEDD • ELMET • POWYS • DUMNONIA

It was from these kingdoms that the fight back against the Saxons was launched ...

ARTHUR LEGEND!
A MOUNTAIN OF MAY-HAVE-BEENS

Of all the leaders of the Britons, the most mysterious is 'King Arthur'. The only certain thing about him is that, if he did exist, he was nothing like the King Arthur of story books!

In 450, when Vortigern, the 'proud tyrant', made the big mistake of inviting Hengist and Horsa to Kent, the British seem to have been divided into two parties. One side *may have been* led by Vortigern. The other side *may have been* led by 'the last of the Romans', a nobleman called Ambrosius Aurelianus. And Arthur *may have been* a war leader for Ambrosius' party.

But although Arthur is lost in the darkest days of the Dark Ages, he is mentioned in a few scraps of early parchments ...

'HE WAS NO ARTHUR'

In 593, after a year of feasting, a band of brave British warriors set out from the hall of Din Eidyn (modern Edinburgh) in the British Kingdom of the Gododdin in southern Scotland. Their tragic story is told in a long, sad poem 'Y Gododdin' by the British poet Aneirin. Aneirin himself rode with the heroes on their 'rough-maned horses like swans'.

The warriors' mission was to attack the stronghold of Catterick which had been captured by a brutal Saxon king called Aethelfrith the Ferocious. The raid was a disaster and most of the British warriors were killed.

But the really interesting thing about this poem is that it says of the leader of the British band that 'he was no Arthur', meaning he wasn't a very good leader. This is the first ever mention of King Arthur and shows that people of that time knew that he was a famous British war leader.

Not every one thought Arthur was a hero. Other British poems are quite rude about him:

The Three Wicked Uncoverings blames Arthur for the conquest of the British by the Saxons, because he took the head of the pagan Celtic god Bran from Tower Hill in London. Bran was meant to protect the British against foreign invasion. Perhaps this poem was written by a Briton who was still a pagan.

The Three Red Ravagers describes Arthur as a curse on Britain and a bit stupid.

SAXONS SLAUGHTERED SHOCK!

It's unlikely that Arthur was stupid. Nennius the Welsh monk tells us that Arthur was a war leader who fought twelve victorious battles against the Saxons. The first was in Lincolnshire, several were in Scotland, one was near Chester, and the last and most important was at a place called 'Mount Badon', which was probably near Bath. In this battle, which must have taken place around AD 500, *'there fell in one onslaught of Arthur's 960 men and none slew them but he alone'*.

After the Battle of Mount Badon the Saxons had to run for it. Many left for the mainland of Europe where they were given land by a German king. The German region of Saxony may be named after them.

And the Britons settled down to enjoy years of peace and plenty ...

CRAZY KINGDOMS

KINGS AND THEIR COMPANIONS

WE'RE BACK!

> Peace and Saxons went together like custard and cabbage. By AD 550 Saxons were back on the warpath all over England. Britain was in for more than two hundred years of warfare.

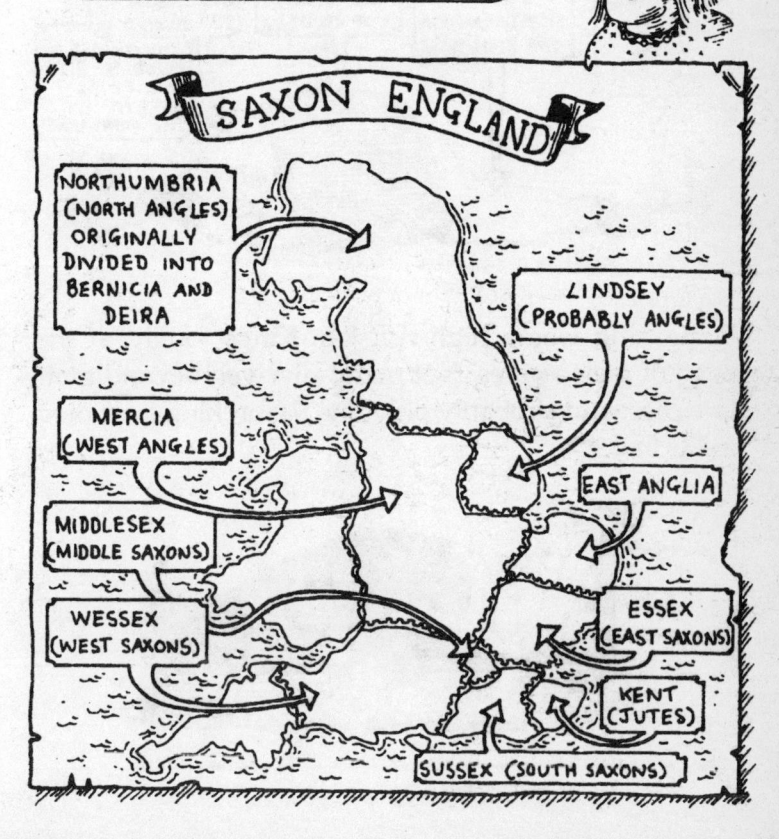

SAXON ENGLAND

- NORTHUMBRIA (NORTH ANGLES) ORIGINALLY DIVIDED INTO BERNICIA AND DEIRA
- LINDSEY (PROBABLY ANGLES)
- MERCIA (WEST ANGLES)
- EAST ANGLIA
- MIDDLESEX (MIDDLE SAXONS)
- WESSEX (WEST SAXONS)
- ESSEX (EAST SAXONS)
- KENT (JUTES)
- SUSSEX (SOUTH SAXONS)

THE KING THING

Kings were top of the Saxon heap. It was Saxons who first introduced coronations to England. But not all kings were equal: little kings were subject to bigger kings, and usually one extra-powerful king made himself *Bretwalda* or 'Britain ruler' and was top king of everybody and his kingdom became the top kingdom. Under-kings had to fight for their masters if called upon.

KINGDOM THING

450 - EARLY SCRAPPY BIT WITH INVASIONS

600 - NORTHUMBRIA TOP KINGDOM

750 - MERCIA TOP KINGDOM

850 - WESSEX TOP KINGDOM

1000-1066 MUDDLED BIT AND FINAL DEFEAT BY THE NORMANS

Being king was a high-risk job. Kings fought at the head of their armies. Not many survived beyond their twenties, and probably only one Saxon king ever died in his bed.

Oswy, king of Northumbria 642-71.

Kings did not inherit their crowns from their fathers. Saxons chose their kings either for life or simply to lead them during a particular war. One way of counting the votes was by a *wapentake*. The warriors held up their weapons and the weapons were counted. The German Franks used to lift up the new king on his shield to show their choice, and perhaps the ancient Saxons did the same.

Any male member of the royal family could be chosen; it was a case of the best man for the job. The one thing he had to have was royal blood. In fact royal blood wasn't enough. To be a king you had to prove that you were descended from a god! All except one of the Saxon royal families claimed to be descended from the god *Woden* at a time before they came to England.

> THE ORIGIN OF THE KINGS OF NORTHUMBRIA
> Woden begot Beldeg, begot Beornec
> begot Gechbrond, begot Aluson,
> and so on ...

East Saxon kings claimed descent from the German god Saxnot, the 'Sword Bearer'.

Means: Woden was the father of Beldeg, who was the father of Beornec etc.

SUTTON WHO? NO, SUTTON *HOO*

Saxon kings could get stinking rich with wealth looted from the British, and wealth given as tribute by lesser chiefs and kings.

They showed off their wealth with precious objects. Saxon craftsmen were very skilful. The greatest hoard of Saxon treasure ever found was excavated in 1938-9 from a field at *Sutton Hoo* in Suffolk. The treasure was buried inside a ship which was then covered in earth. There was no body, and the burial is thought to be a monument to Raedwald, king of the East Angles and Bretwalda of southern England around AD 600 who may have died at sea or abroad.

The Sutton Hoo treasures include gold and silver jewellery, a sword, a harp, a Roman dish, armour and a helmet.

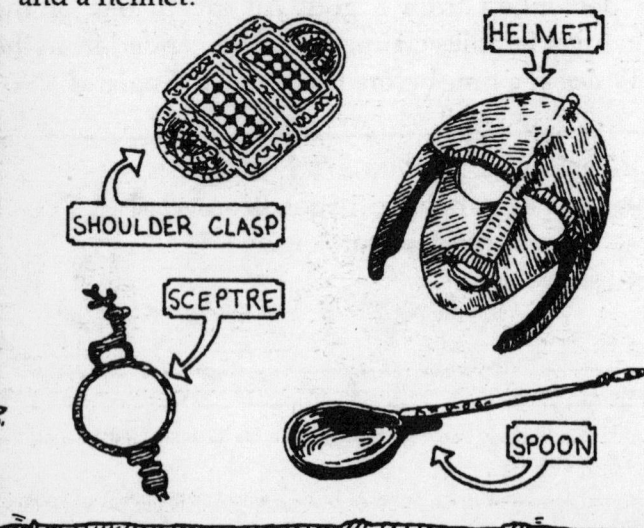

FEELING COMPANIONABLE?

Every German king, including Saxon kings, lived with a group of faithful 'companions' called *thegns* 🦶 or *gesith*. These were young warriors of noble blood. They lived in the king's hall, feasted with him and fought beside him. The Roman writer Tacitus says that, when not fighting, companions did nothing except drink and enjoy themselves. They were too lazy even to hunt. Kings were often known as 'ring-givers'. They had to win battles and to give their companions expensive presents in order to keep their support.

The worst thing a companion could do was to leave a battle alive after his king had been killed. As one Saxon poet 🦶 put it:

> *Our spirits shall be sterner, hearts the keener*
> *Courage the greater, as our strength fades.*
> *Here on the ground lies our lord, a good man cut down.*
> *The man who thinks of leaving the battle now will*
> *regret it for ever.*

🦶 Pronounced *thayns*.

🦶 His poem is called *The Battle of Maldon*. It describes a battle which a band of Saxons lost to Vikings in the tenth century.

Tall halls

All the feasting and fun took place in the lord or king's hall. To this day the big house in many villages is called the 'hall'.

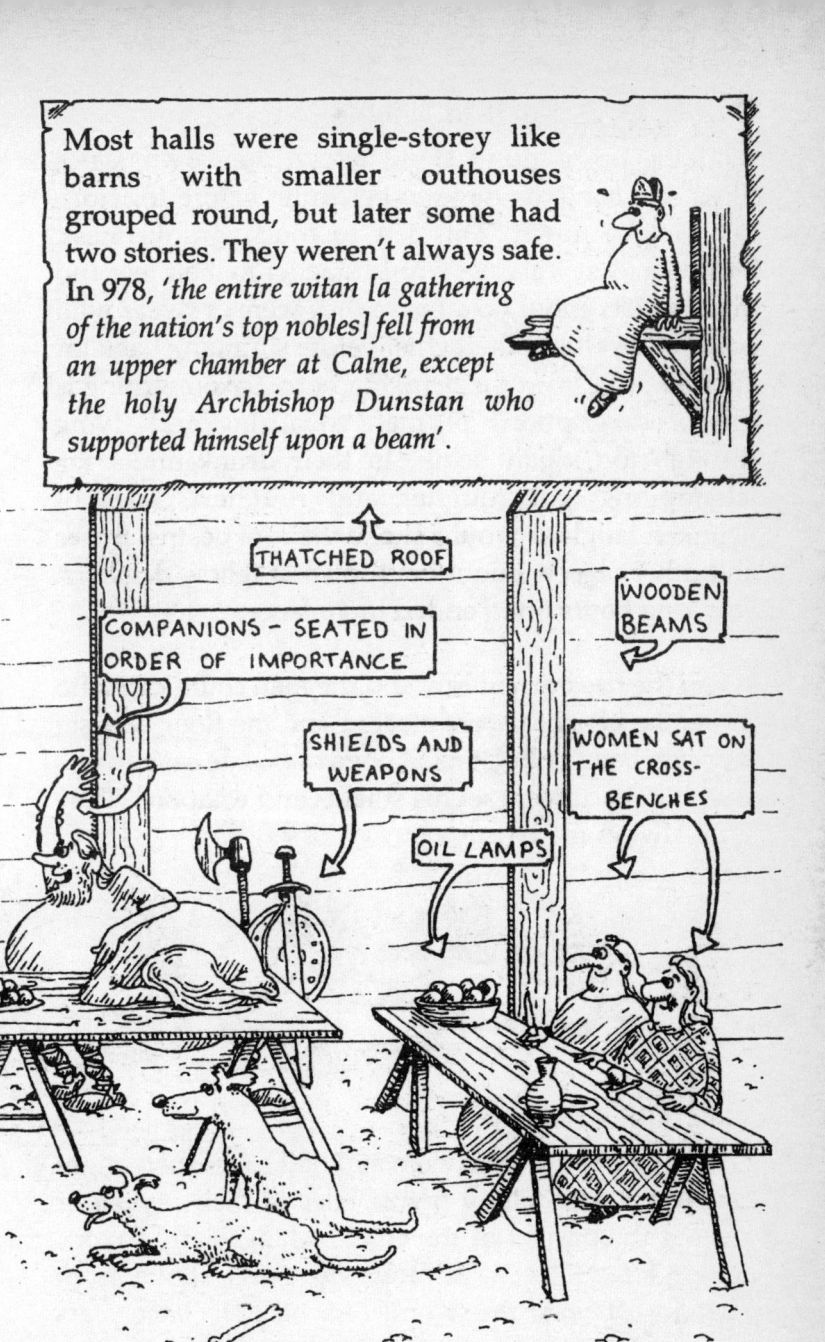

Most halls were single-storey like barns with smaller outhouses grouped round, but later some had two stories. They weren't always safe. In 978, *'the entire witan [a gathering of the nation's top nobles] fell from an upper chamber at Calne, except the holy Archbishop Dunstan who supported himself upon a beam'.*

THATCHED ROOF

WOODEN BEAMS

COMPANIONS - SEATED IN ORDER OF IMPORTANCE

SHIELDS AND WEAPONS

WOMEN SAT ON THE CROSS-BENCHES

OIL LAMPS

DRUNK AS A SKUNK IN A BUNK

Drinking horns don't stand up on their own. Once filled, the contents have to be drunk before the horn can be put down. This led to much drunkenness. During a feast warriors would stagger to their feet and make boasts about how brave they were or swear wild oaths of loyalty to their chief before slumping back for another swig from the drinking horn. Saxon writing is full of descriptions of men collapsing and dying through too much drink. In their drunkenness the 'champions' got rougher and rougher. Gales of drunken laughter would shake the roof beams. Bones and other objects might be thrown at fellow drinkers. Drinking bouts often ended in violence.

When the fire burned low and the men could drink no more, the benches were cleared and the floor was set out with beds or bolsters. Above or beside each man's sleeping place were set his shields and weapons. They were always ready for war.

TIME FOR A TUNE

While the companions were still half sober they might listen to a poet telling heroic tales of their people or singing the praises of the chief or king. Early Saxons couldn't read or write and the poets spoke from memory, often to the sound of a harp. In later years one of these poems was written down ...

BEOWULF

Beowulf is one of the oldest poems written in English. It tells the story of a hero, Beowulf, of the Swedish tribe of the Geats, who sailed to Denmark to the hall of a Danish king.

A man-eating monster called Grendel had caused trouble, carrying off the king's companions at night while they slept and then eating them: 'By morning all the bench-boards would be drenched with blood' as the poet puts it. While staying in the hall, Beowulf wrestled with Grendel and pulled off one of its arms so that the monster died in agony.

But that's not the end of the story. Grendel's mum came along to get her own back. Beowulf had to kill Mum as well, tracking her to her underwater cave. 'The sword took her hard on the neck and broke the rings of bone; the broad sword passed straight through her death-doomed flesh. She fell to the floor. The sword was gory,' says the poet.

KING THING - AGAIN

One of these things has been chosen to be king. Which one is it?

Answer: The one on the shield

A FEW THINGS TO DO WITHOUT DRINKING

The companions did have a few other activities apart from drinking, boasting and fighting.

Gambling: Germans, including early Saxons, were so fond of gambling that men would even bet themselves on a throw of the dice, becoming slaves if they lost.

PLACE YOUR BETS

I AM MY BET!

Caroles: the Saxons and the British both liked caroles, which were a mixture of singing and dancing.

But there's no doubt that singing, dancing, gambling, and even drinking, came a very poor second to fighting as the companions' favourite activity. After all that's what the king needed them for.

FIVE PENCE PER FINGER!

Paw laws ...

Price of power

Among Saxons, the more important you were, the higher your price or *wergild*. Wergild was the money that had to be paid to a victim's family if you killed or wronged him or her in some way. The wergild for a nobleman was much higher than for a *churl*, or free peasant. Slaves had no wergild at all, although if you killed one you still had to pay his or her owner the price of about eight oxen.

WESSEX WERGILD

SLAVES – NOTHING WORTH SPEAKING OF

CHURLS OR CEORLS (FREE PEASANTS) – 200 SHILLINGS

NOBLE WARRIOR COMPANIONS, CALLED THEGNS OR GESITH – 600 SHILLINGS

KING OR CHIEF – THE SKY'S THE LIMIT!

Wergild means 'man-price'.

The highest wergilds were paid out for murder, but there were plenty of other crimes carefully spelled out in the laws of different Saxon kings. You might pay five pence for the finger of a churl and twenty pence for the finger of a thegn. Here are the payments which would be due to a churl's family in Wessex under King Alfred the Great:

SIXTY SHILLINGS FOR A NOSE

TWENTY SHILLINGS FOR A BIG TOE

THIRTY SHILLINGS FOR AN EAR STRUCK OFF

FOUR SHILLINGS FOR A BACK TOOTH KNOCKED OUT

Thegns were noble, churls were commoners - but not too common. In the early days a churl could hope to become a thegn: it all depended on land. A *hide* of land was enough to support one family. If a churl could get his hands on at least five hides, he could become a thegn. Later the thegns grew more powerful and they made the churls work for them. It became almost impossible to move from one class to another.

A shilling was worth twelve old pence. It was in use until 1971 when it was abolished. In Saxon times a shilling was worth a lot.

WEIGH YOUR WORDS!

Under the laws of King Alfred, if you could persuade 'twelve king's thegns' to swear that you were innocent of murder - then you were innocent! Oaths were all you needed. You could do the same with churls, but you would need more of them, because just as different classes had different wergilds, so they also had different 'strengths' of oath. The oath of a thegn counted for more than the oath of a churl.

Gradually a system of law courts grew up, based on *hundreds*, which were areas of land often the size of a *hundred* hides. Hundred courts met in the open air about once a month. All churls took part in their local court.

The meeting place for a hundred court was called a moot.

Ow!

If no one would swear for you, you might choose to rely on God to prove your innocence. 'Trial by ordeal' was a painful way of asking God for his opinion. It was especially popular once the Saxons became Christian (more on that later). Here's one form of ordeal - but don't try this at home if you know what's good for you!

1. Plunge your hand into a cauldron of boiling water up to the wrist or elbow and pick up a stone from the bottom.

2. Carry the stone 2.7 metres.

3. Bandage your hand.

4. Three days later unwrap the bandage. If your damaged hand is not infected, then you're innocent. God has proved it by helping to heal you.

DUEL!

Another way for God to settle a case was by a duel, or 'trial by combat'. The idea was that God would help the person who was in the right. Women and old people could choose a champion to fight for them. Duellists took it in turn to strike each other and the idea was to strike a few very powerful blows. Before any duel there was always a long argument over who should strike first. It could make a big difference, although not always. Take this description of a duellist's blow during a fight between two champions called Agnarus and Biarco:

> *Agnarus cut through the front of the helmet, wounded the skin of the scalp and had to let go of his sword which became locked in the vizor holes ... then Biarco passed his fine-edged blade through the midst of Agnarus' body. Agnarus, in supreme suppression of his pain gave up the ghost with his lips relaxed into a smile.*

MMMPHFF!

Painful punishments

Imagine you've been found guilty and now it's time for punishment. You can't afford to pay any wergild and you'll just have to suffer. There's no proper prison because there are no stone buildings worth speaking of - unless you count being shut up in a shed with your hands and feet tied up while you wait for trial.

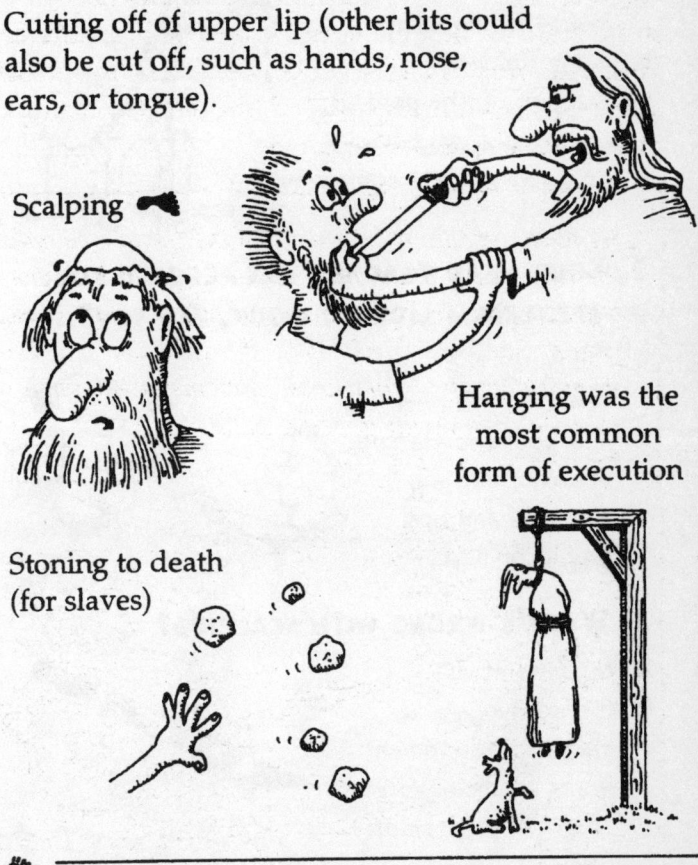

Cutting off of upper lip (other bits could also be cut off, such as hands, nose, ears, or tongue).

Scalping

Hanging was the most common form of execution

Stoning to death (for slaves)

First used by the Saxons, as far as is known. Later, in the seventeenth century, English soldiers were paid £5 per head for dead Irish rebels. Heads were heavy so they took *scalps* instead. When English soldiers were sent to America, native Americans learned scalping from them.

IT'S THE LAW!

Check it out - are you the right type to be a seriously savage Saxon?
Part 3

1. WHAT IS A WERGILD?

a. A trade union that only meets by moonlight
b. A type of wolf
c. The price to be paid to someone if you have wronged them in some way

2. YOUR HEAD TEACHER HAS ACCUSED YOU OF STEALING A LIBRARY BOOK. DO YOU?..

a. Challenge the head teacher to a duel
b. Ask your friends to speak up for you
c. Start crying and say it isn't fair

3. WHAT'S WRONG WITH SCALPING?

a. Nothing at all
b. It's a savage and barbaric punishment
c. It's a bit messy and the knife gets blunt

Answers on page 121

CALL OUT THE SHERIFF!

There were no policemen in Saxon times. In fact there was so little law and order that one law ordered all travellers to carry horns to blow if ever they wandered off the beaten track - to warn people that they were coming so as to show that they weren't thieves!

There were no policemen, but there were *sheriffs*. English counties, or *shires*, were started by the Saxons and the king's official in each shire came to be called a *reeve*. Put the two together and you get *shire-reeve*, or 'sheriff'. The sheriff was a major figure in the shire court, which tried cases which were too important for the hundreds courts. The sheriff was important, but the local *ealdorman*, later known as an 'earl' was even more important. *Ealdormen* were nobles who controlled the shires.

POWER TOWER

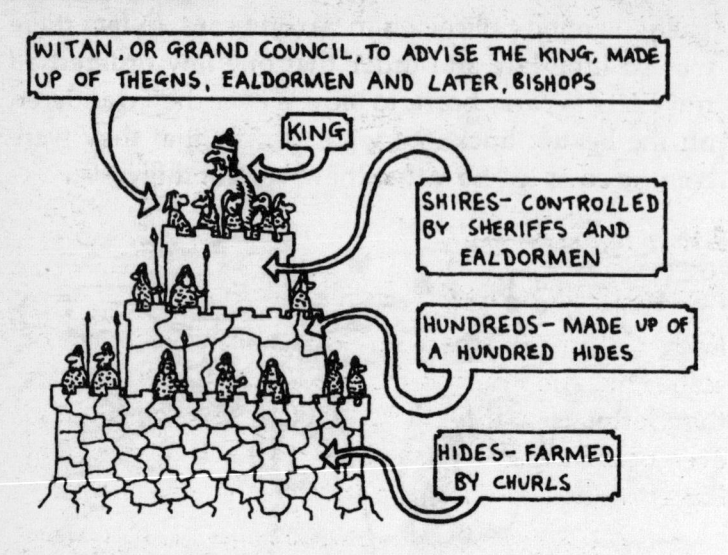

WITAN, OR GRAND COUNCIL, TO ADVISE THE KING, MADE UP OF THEGNS, EALDORMEN AND LATER, BISHOPS

KING

SHIRES - CONTROLLED BY SHERIFFS AND EALDORMEN

HUNDREDS - MADE UP OF A HUNDRED HIDES

HIDES - FARMED BY CHURLS

Churls were the foundation blocks of Saxon society. As long as the churls kept farming their hides of land, the tower would not topple over ...

DOWN ON THE FARM

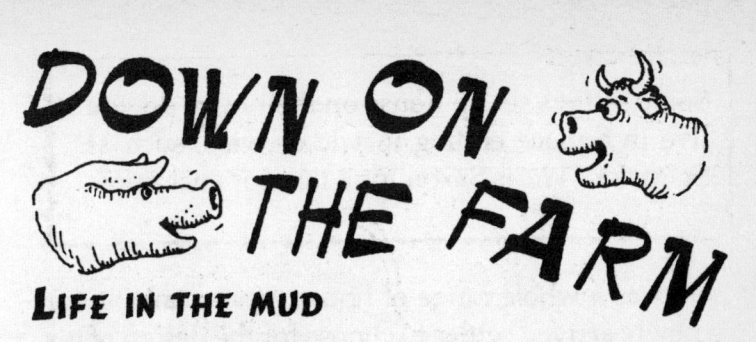

LIFE IN THE MUD

FROWNS FOR TOWNS

Early Saxons frowned on towns. Towns were for softies like the Romano-Britons. According to Tacitus, the Germans, which included the Saxons, couldn't even bear houses built in rows: *'they live apart, each by himself, as woodside, plain, or fresh spring attracts him'*.

Most of the warriors and their families who came to Britain built their first grubby huts in the countryside. Only a few set up camp among the stone ruins of the cities, ruins which some Saxons thought were the work of giants.

> Some settlers set up house on their own: do you live in a place ending in wic or wick, such as Stanwick? *Wic* is Saxon for a farm or enclosure.

There was a whole range of house types available for the newly arrived settler to choose for the design of his building:

small pit-huts, often used as storage sheds

larger pit-huts used as houses

small halls with plank walls

great hall for chiefs

STRIP OFF AND START WORK

Having built their houses, they set out to farm the land, using the 'open field' system. Open fields were not fields with the gate left open; they were two or three huge fields farmed by all the people of a village. The fields were divided into narrow *strips* and each family received a number of strips to farm. Every year one field was left *fallow* - without crops growing on it - so that the soil could recover its fertility.

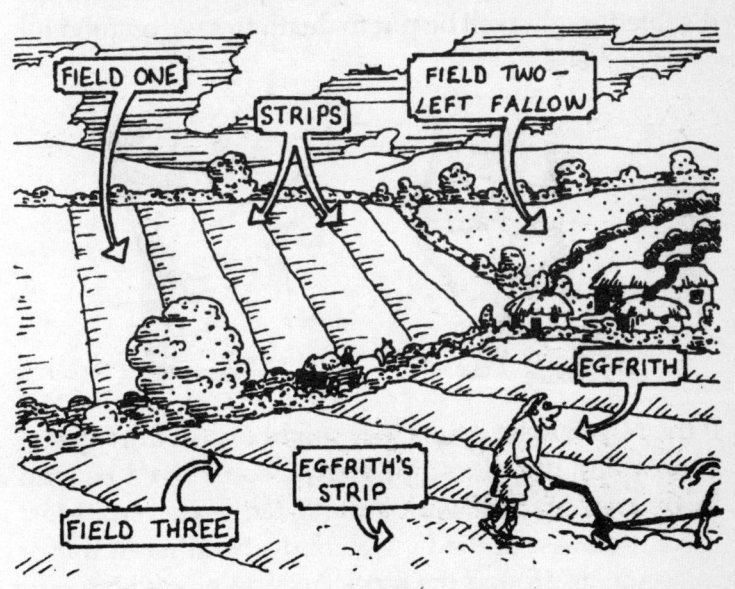

The life of a churl was hard, and got harder, even if he had a slave or two to help him. In early Saxon times his duty was to give food-rent direct to the king and to fight for him in battle. In later years, as the thegns grew more powerful, churls paid tribute to their local lords in the form of labour. A *cottar* for instance was a poor peasant who worked for his lord

---

Slaves cost roughly twice as much as horses.

each Monday and three days a week at harvest time – which left three days per week to harvest his own strips. When the Saxons became Christians, a cottar working on Sunday could be fined sixty shillings. If he couldn't pay it he might be made into a slave. Life was definitely better in the early days.

ELF TROUBLE

Most Saxons didn't live very long. The sick and the disabled might well be put to death to save on food for everyone else.

If they lived to be adults they might expect thirty years of working life, since not many people lived beyond forty (they started work around ten years old). Most died of disease or died a violent death either in war or in accidents around the farm. Around twenty per cent of Saxons suffered from broken bones.

Saxons believed in elves. They thought that illness was caused by evil elves who shot darts into their victims. The elves had to be driven out, which makes some of their ideas for treatment seem pretty basic:

'if a horse is elf-shot, whatever elf is involved this will cure him ... take a stick, strike him on the back.'

Working on the same principle, people with mental problems were beaten and cattle were driven through smoke to drive out evil.

Not all cures were so unpleasant. Bathing was meant to be good for health, although it wasn't something that Saxons liked to do too much of. They made steam baths by pouring water on to hot stones, or they could *'sleep next to a fat child'* as a way of keeping warm.

FOOD FOR THOUGHT

The main crops were wheat, rye, barley, beans and oats. Saxons slopped these down as porridge, cakes, bread and other simple foods. There was also meat, much of it slaughtered in autumn and then preserved by salting, thus saving on winter fodder. They even ate horse meat, although this was banned after 787. By that time the Saxons had become Christian and eating horse meat was thought to be a pagan custom.

There were other special laws about what you could eat. How about this law of King Edgar:

> *'if a hen drink human blood, it is lawful to eat it after three months.'* Meaning it was forbidden to eat the hen for three months after it drank the blood.

> Hens that drank human blood - where did they find the blood?! Does it make you wonder what life was really like down on the farm?

A RUMBLE WITH THE THUNDER GOD

YOU MAY BE MORE OF A PAGAN THAN YOU THOUGHT!

IT'S A DEAD CERTAINTY

Pagan Saxons did not fear death - or at least they tried not to show they did. They believed that the moment of their death was decided by three 'fates' before they were born. The fates were three women - representing the past, present and future - who lived beneath the great circle of the Earth.

> YOU CAN HAVE A WONDERFUL LIFE WITH LOTS OF MONEY AND LIVE TO A HUNDRED.

> YOU CAN HAVE A HORRIBLE, MISERABLE LIFE AND DIE BEFORE YOU'RE TWENTY.

HUMAN SOULS

WAY OUT

Since the time of a Saxon's death was already decided, there was no point in worrying about it. *'Fearlessness is better than a faint heart for any man who puts his nose out of doors. The length of my life and the day of my death were fated long ago'* as one poet put it.

Warriors especially needed to be brave - Woden was waiting for them.

WATCH OUT FOR WODEN!

Saxons gods were the gods of the north, the same gods as those worshipped by the pagan Germans and later by the Vikings. Greatest of all the northern gods was *Woden*, called *Odin* by the Vikings in later years.

Woden was dangerous. He wandered the world in disguise collecting the souls of warriors slain in battle. He stirred up trouble between people because more battles meant more dead warriors. He needed their souls to fight beside him in a great battle which would take place at the end of the world, a battle between the gods and the forces of darkness in which both the gods and their enemies would all die.

ONE EYE — WODEN — MAGIC SPEAR — BLUE CLOAK — TWO RAVENS, BIRDS OF BATTLE, (NORMALLY SAT ON HIS SHOULDER)

Woden tended to be worshipped by warriors, but *Thunor*, called *Thor* by the Vikings, was popular among churls. He was a huge red-haired god who carried a hammer and made thunder. He was more trustworthy than Woden.

AND WATCH OUT FOR WEDNESBURY!

Only Woden accepted human sacrifices. Sacrificial victims might be first strangled, then thrown into bogs or lakes. Others were hung from trees in 'sacred groves'. Many places in England were centres of Woden worship: watch out for names like *Wednesfield* or 'Woden's Field' and *Wednesbury*, meaning 'Woden's fortress'.

But if you live in one of these places, there's no need for any human sacrifices!

URGSPLFF!!

Pagan places

Many of us live near pagan shrines and sanctuaries. Mostly Saxons worshipped their gods outdoors by sacred trees, springs or boundaries, although sometimes they built temples which seem to have looked a bit like large farmhouses. *Wih* or *weoh* meant an idol or shrine: does your town or village have a name like 'Weedon' or 'Wheeley'?

Or does it sound a bit like someone clearing their throat? *'Hearh'* meant a 'sacred place on a hill'. Names like *Harrow* come from it. In fact Harrow was the largest centre of pagan worship in the country. Much blood must have flowed from the sacrifices at Harrow.

HEARH HEARH

Cuthwulf's calendar

There was a whole year of god worship and sacrificing for Saxons to get through, starting on 25 December which was the pagan New Year. Take these three Saxon months:

Halgmonath
Month of offerings, or 'holy month'.

Blotmonath
Month of blood or sacrifice, when animals were slaughtered before winter.

Solomonath
During the second month, known as the 'month of cakes', cakes were offered to the gods.

Not all the months were for the gods: During *Thrimilci* cows were 'milked three times' a day. *Weodmonath* was the month of weeds.

FANCY SOME CHOCOLATE?

Do you like eating chocolate Easter eggs and Easter bunnies? Nowadays Easter is a Christian festival celebrating Christ's return from the dead after his crucifixion - but it has another history.

Eostre, where the word 'Easter' comes from, was the Saxon goddess of spring and the dawn. The hare was her sacred beast, which is where 'Easter' bunnies come from and Saxon tradition said that the hare was the bringer of eggs during the 'Eostre' festival. Put that in silver paper and eat it!

OH MY GOD!

We still honour the pagan Saxon gods - almost every time we say the name of a day of the week.

> *Sunday* - the day of the Sun
> *Monday* - the day of the Moon
> *Tuesday* - the day of Tiw, god of war
> *Wednesday* - the day of Woden
> *Thursday* - the day of Thunor
> *Friday* - the day of Frig, goddess and wife of Woden
> *Saturday* - all right, so this one isn't Saxon, but it's still sacred to a god - Saturn, the Roman god of agriculture!

There were gods and magic monsters everywhere. There were the elves who caused illnesses, and two types of giant, the *ents* who built great buildings and *thyrs*, who were - just giants.

Also there were dragons which guarded the treasure in old burial mounds and monsters which lived in wild, desolate places. Do you know anyone who looks like this? If so, perhaps they're descended from a Saxon monster ...

'great head, long neck, thin face, horse teeth, throat vomiting flames, twisted jaw, thick lips, strident voice, pigeon breast, scabby thighs, knotty knees, crooked ankles, splay feet ...'

Pagan Saxon religion was always interesting.

ANGELS AND DEVILS

TAMING THE PAGANS

DO WE HAVE TO?!

Around the year AD 577. A Christian priest walks past the slave market in Rome and sees some fair-haired children up for sale. He asks who they are and is told that they are Angles from Britain. 'These are not Angles,' he says: 'They're angels!'.

THESE ARE NOT ANGLES!

From that day on he nurses the ambition to convert all the Angles and Saxons in Britain to Christianity.

Twenty years later that same monk becomes Pope Gregory I, known as 'the Great'. Now that he's Pope he wants to travel to Britain to convert the Angles, but, being Pope, he has to stay in Rome. So instead he asks a monk called Augustine to go to Britain for him.

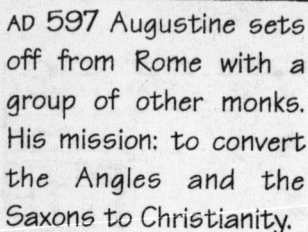

AD 597 Augustine sets off from Rome with a group of other monks. His mission: to convert the Angles and the Saxons to Christianity.

The further they travel, the more nervous the monks become at the thought of meeting all those pagan Saxons. Half way across France they send a message back to Gregory, begging him not to make them go on.

Gregory insists that they continue.

Later in AD 597, Augustine lands in Kent.

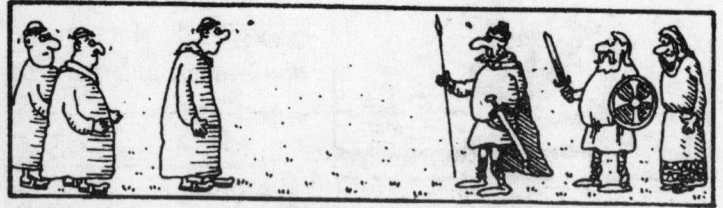

Augustine meets the pagan King Aethelberht of Kent. The king is so afraid of the strangers' magic that he will only meet Augustine out of doors.

Augustine and his monks are allowed to stay in Canterbury and preach to the Saxons.

CUNNING CHRISTIANS

Wherever the missionaries preached they first planted a cross to drive out pagan spirits. But they had to tread carefully and not offend any pagan warriors, who would have been more than happy to slice up the missionaries with their swords.

> WOULD YOU MIND AWFULLY IF I ACTUALLY REALLY JUST PREACHED A TINY BIT ABOUT CHRISTIANITY? IF YOU DON'T MIND...

Before the Battle of Chester in 616 Aethelfrith the Ferocious massacred 1,200 monks. They had been praying for the enemy, and as Aethelfrith put it:

'If they pray to their God against us, they too, unarmed as they are, are fighting against us.'

In other words: they had it coming.

A BIGGER SPLASH

The missionaries worked very carefully indeed. First they converted the kings and thegns, then the ordinary people followed. On one occasion ten thousand were converted on a single day! The process of conversion involved being totally dunked in a pond or river so there must have been a lot of wet Saxons sloshing around that day.

Even after large numbers of Saxons had become Christians the missionaries took no chances. They built their churches on pagan sacred sites, following orders from Pope Gregory in a letter from Rome:

'the temples of the idols in that nation [England] ought not to be destroyed, but let the idols that are in them be destroyed ... that the people may resort to the places to which they have been accustomed'.

In this way the Saxons would not feel that their ancient customs were completely lost. And that's why most churches in England are built on pagan sacred sites.

The pagans weren't taking too many chances either - even after they'd been converted! Raedwald, the king of East Anglia whose memorial was probably buried at Sutton Hoo, kept two altars in the same temple - one for Christ, and one at which he offered sacrifices to 'devils'!

PERSUADING THE PAGANS

Compared to Woden and human sacrifice, you might think that Christianity would seem rather too tame to a pagan. Why should any self-respecting Woden-worshipper want to change his or her religion?

Well they did. Edwin, king of Northumbria from 617 - 633, was a pagan when he married the Christian daughter of the king of Kent. She brought a missionary called Paulinus with her when she came to Edwin, and Paulinus argued with Edwin and his thegns in Edwin's great hall. After Paulinus had urged

Edwin and his pagan companions to become Christians, an unnamed pagan thegn described the hopelessness of human life. This is a shortened version of what he said:

> *The life of man, O king, seems to me like the flight of a sparrow through the room where you sit, flying in at one door and out at another. It appears for a short space, but of what went before or what is to follow, we are utterly ignorant. If this new doctrine contains something more certain, it deserves to be followed.*

In other words: Christianity seemed to offer the hope of life after death - and Paulinus sounded so convincing!

Paulinus converted the Northumbrians lock, stock and barrel. Pagan priests were not allowed to carry weapons or ride stallions, but Coifi, Edwin's pagan priest, borrowed weapons, jumped on a stallion, and rode thirty-two kilometres to the pagan shrine at Goodmanham. In front of a crowd which thought he was crazy he threw a spear into the shrine and called on his companions to burn it down! Which they did.

A PAUSE FOR PENDA, THE 'LAST OF THE PAGANS'

Christianity spread fast, but some pagans were prepared to resist it. Some were even prepared to make friends with Christians in order to fight Christianity!

AD 626. A year before Edwin is baptized in the city of York, a ruthless war-leader called Penda is chosen to be king of the Mercians who live in the Midlands. Penda will rule for thirty bloody years.

AD 632. Penda and the Christian British king Caedwalla of North Wales join forces and march on Saxon Northumbria in an unholy combination of wild pagans and Christians.

Later in 632. Edwin is killed by Penda and Caedwalla at the battle of Haethfield. The plain of Haethfield 'reeks with human blood'.

Caedwalla is a Christian but with the heart of a pagan. He is filled with hatred of the Saxons and intends to drive them from England. He shows no mercy to man, woman or child in Northumbria.

> Because of Caedwalla and Penda the Northumbrians went back to being pagans for many years. Christianity spread fast, but the old gods didn't give up without a struggle.

WE'RE STILL AROUND!

BRITISH BELIEVERS

... AND THEIR MONKEY BUSINESS

NORTHERN DISCOMFORTS

Even during the darkest days at the end of the Roman Empire, Christianity had survived in England - but only just. It had clung on like a man hanging from a window-sill by his fingertips - and pagan Saxons had behaved like someone trying to stamp on his fingers! Around the edges of England - in Wales, Scotland, Cornwall and Ireland - it was Celtic Britons who had kept the flame of Christianity alive.

You just can't keep a good religion down! Paganism was caught in a pincer movement. To the south Augustine's missionaries argued them into submission, and in the north and west there were a few brave Celtic Christians to do the same ...

> TAKE FOR INSTANCE THE BOOK OF ECCLESIASTES IN THE BIBLE, CHAPTER ONE, VERSE TWO BLAH, BLAH, BLAH...
>
> NO, PLEASE, STOP!

During the Saxon period Cornwall was inhabited by British Celts and so was not part of England.

The Celtic Christianity of the Britons was different from the Roman Christianity of Augustine. Celtic monks lived in small, individual cells 🐾 . They believed in poverty and loneliness and often wandered off into the wide blue yonder, *'going into exile for the love of God, it mattered not whither'*. Later they reached Iceland and there were even tales that a Celtic monk called Brendan sailed as far as America in a small boat, searching for solitude.

ROCK AND SOUL

Off the west coast of Scotland there's a lump of rock about two kilometres long. It's an island, called Iona, and it's incredibly old, older than the beginning of life

> Their cells were small bare rooms but, unlike prison cells, they often stood alone with their own walls and roof.

on Earth, so old that there are no fossils in it. The Celts believed that Iona had been forged at the beginning of the world and would be the last place to be destroyed on the Day of Doom.

No wonder that Celtic monks built a monastery there.

It was on the Celtic island of Iona that Oswald, the next great Saxon king of Northumbria after Edwin, was educated.

After he had become king of Northumbria, Oswald asked the Celtic monks of Iona to send missionaries to Northumbria. The Celts sent a bishop called Aidan. Aidan didn't like Saxons and he couldn't speak the language, but he went anyway and in 635 founded a monastery on the island of Lindisfarne just off the coast of Northumbria.

Lindisfarne was run in the Celtic style. The monks had little cells and lived lives of poverty. Any money they received from the rich they immediately gave to the poor. They also celebrated Easter on a different day to everyone else, which may not seem very important nowadays - but it was then.

ANOTHER PAUSE FOR PENDA

So now the *Saxon* Northumbrians had become *Celtic* Christians. They had their own little rocky monastery, Lindisfarne, just like rocky Celtic Iona. In fact they might have stayed Celtic Christians for ever, except for one problem. This problem had a capital P and that P stood for ...

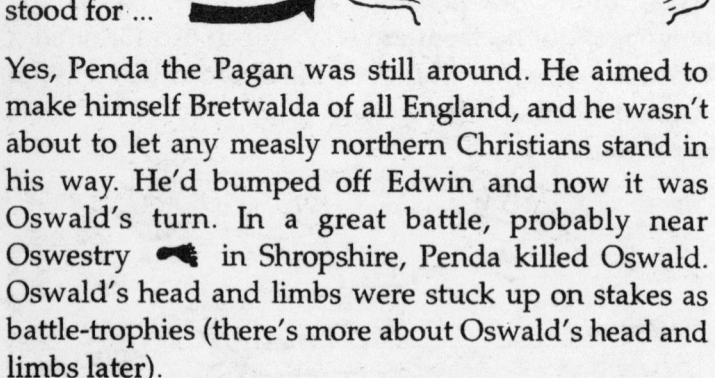

Yes, Penda the Pagan was still around. He aimed to make himself Bretwalda of all England, and he wasn't about to let any measly northern Christians stand in his way. He'd bumped off Edwin and now it was Oswald's turn. In a great battle, probably near Oswestry in Shropshire, Penda killed Oswald. Oswald's head and limbs were stuck up on stakes as battle-trophies (there's more about Oswald's head and limbs later).

The town name *Oswestry* may come from 'Oswald's Tree', meaning the place where Oswald raised his standard.

O. Bros. - A Short Interval

Saxon names within a family often started with the same letter. Oswald's brother, who followed him shortly after as king of Northumbria was called Oswy. Some of the 'Oses' in the picture below were pagan and some were Christian, but they were all members of the Northumbrian royal family. Can you pick out the pagans? (Answer upside down).

Answer: You can't tell the Christian from the pagans in this picture. Christian Saxons could be just as warlike as pagan Saxons.

LITTLE THINGS AND BIG THINGS

People in different periods of history have different ways of looking at the world.

Little things: in the modern world, chopping someone's head off with a sword is considered quite a big thing. Among the Anglo-Saxons it was a quite little thing because it happened all the time.

Big things: in the modern world, the date when we have our Easter holiday is quite a little thing - at least compared to murdering people. Among the Anglo-Saxons the date of Easter was a very big thing indeed.

In 642 Oswy was king of Northumbria. He was a Christian like his late lamented brother Oswald. There was only one cloud on his horizon. Oswy was married to a West Saxon princess who followed the Roman system of Christianity and not the Celtic system as Oswy did: this meant (shock horror) that husband and wife celebrated Easter on different days, because of the different ways that the Celtic and Roman churches worked out when Easter should be 🐾.

Something had to be done.

He celebrated Easter on 14 April and she celebrated it on 21 April that year.

Oswy called a grand meeting of Roman and Celtic Christians. It was held at Whitby in Yorkshire in 664 and has been known ever since as the 'Synod of Whitby'. There were two matters to clear up:

1 Haircuts
2 The date of Easter

The tonsure was a way of cutting the hair of priests. Celtic Christians shaved the front half of their heads; Roman Christians like Augustine shaved a circular patch in the middle. How to wear your tonsure was a serious question in those days, but the question of the date of Easter was even more important.

The Roman Christians, led by an angry abbot called Wilfred, pointed out that all other Christians in the world agreed with them about Easter, and only the Celtic church disagreed. The poor old Celts who had been busy living in poverty and looking after the poor were no match for Wilfrid's silver tongue.

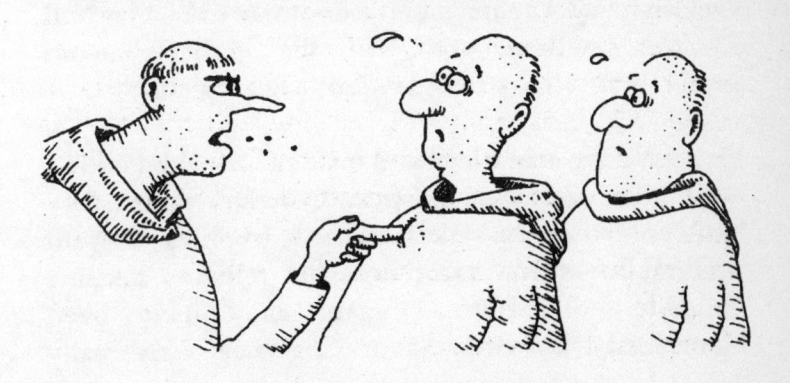

A *synod* is a meeting of important churchmen.

King Oswy asked Wilfrid if the Roman church was founded by Saint Peter 'the keeper of the keys to heaven'. Wilfrid said it was. Oswy then decided that since the Roman church was founded by Saint Peter, he had better follow Peter rather than the Celtic church if he wanted to get into heaven when he died (Oswy is reported to have spoken with a smile).

So the Celtic Christians lost the argument - but they kept their haircuts for a while longer.

YOUNG, HANDSOME CHRISTIAN CHOPS UP GRIZZLED, OLD PAGAN

Christians were popping up everywhere. Even Penda the Last of the Pagans met his doom. In 651 Oswy 'cut off the heathen head' of the eighty-year-old Penda ☛ after a two-day battle near Leeds.

Meantime the arms, legs and head of Oswald, Penda's last victim, were rescued from Oswestry where they had been stuck on stakes as battle-trophies. Oswald was made into a saint and his remains became valuable holy relics. Pagans may have been bloodthirsty, but early Saxon Christians were really

---

At eighty Penda must have been one of the oldest men in England - not bad for a man who had spent most of his life on the warpath.

weird. Take this description of Oswald's head, which was kept at Durham cathedral:

'The roundness of the head, completely spherical, gives off a wonderfully sweet fragrance ... glowing a deep yellow colour which surpasses the yellowness of wax and is closer in its great beauty and loveliness to the appearance of gold ...'

Yes, Christianity had come to the Saxons. Even Penda's son Peada became a Christian.

MORE MONKEY BUSINESS

So maybe you're the right type to be a savage Saxon - but could you have been a glad-to-be-good Saxon? Let's find out - part 1.

1. HOW DID CELTIC MONKS LIKE TO LIVE?

a. In huge monasteries and all crammed into large dormitories at night
b. As far away from people as possible
c. In large libraries with their bunks laid out between the shelves

2. WHAT WAS THE CELTIC TONSURE?

a. A hair style where the front half of the head was shaved
b. A hair style where a round patch on top of the head was shaved
c. A horrible form of scalping reserved for pagans

3. WHAT WAS THE SYNOD OF WHITBY?

a. A meeting of churchmen to decide on the date of Christmas
b. A meeting of churchmen to decide on the date of Easter

Answers on page 121

WISE WOMEN

AND MAD MISSIONARIES
BUT FIRST - SOME *WILD* WOMEN

England had changed. It had thrown away its dirty Dark Age rags and stepped into the satiny silks of civilization (well, not that silky, more woolly and leathery really). Civilization in Europe meant Christianity in those days. In England it was only in Christian cathedrals and monasteries that books were written and ideas were argued over. And right at the front of the writing and arguing were a number of amazing women.

Actually Saxon women, right from the time when they lived in Germany, before they came to England, had always been amazing. Who else except the Germans and Saxons ever called their little girls names like:

Gertrude means 'Spear-Strength'
Hilda means 'Battle Maid'
Griselda means 'Grey Battle Maid'

These were the women whom the Roman writer Tacitus describes as standing behind their men in battle and killing any who fled from the enemy!

But now they turned their talents to doing good.

NUNKS

Question: what do you get when you mix monks with nuns?
Wrong answer: nunks.
Right answer: a double monastery for both monks and nuns. Some were started by rich families as a way to avoid tax (the church didn't have to pay taxes). Many more were started by rich royal women. The very first was a member of the Northumbrian royal family called Hilda. She started the double monastery at Whitby where the famous 'Synod' about haircuts and Easter was held.

Usually the men and women in a double monastery lived totally separate lives. (The Abbess of Wimbourne only gave orders to her monks through a window.) But every now and then things broke down:

The nuns of Coldingham spent their time sewing robes to make themselves look nice - or to give to the men. The nuns and monks had to be separated.

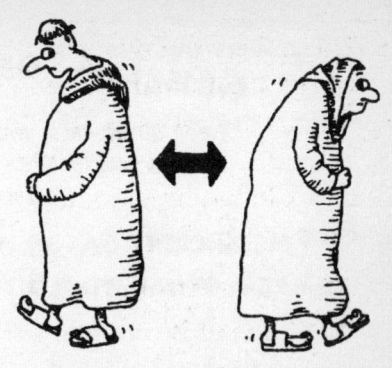

The nuns at Barking had to be warned against satin undergarments, hair arranged with curling irons and jewellery.

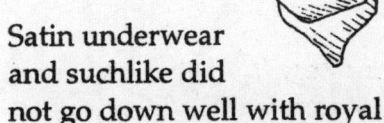

Satin underwear and suchlike did not go down well with royal Christians such as Saint Etheldreda, Abbess of Ely. She didn't even bathe unless she had to!

> Bathing does not seem to have been very popular with saints. Saint Cuthbert used to keep his shoes on from one Easter to the next, only taking them off once a year on Maundy Thursday, the Thursday before Easter, for a ritual foot-washing session!

GRISELDA GETS MAD!

Check it out - are you the right type to be a seriously savage Saxon?
Part 4

1. THIS ANCIENT SAXON WOMAN HAS LOST HER TEMPER. WHAT WOULD YOU DO TO STOP HER?

a. Stand up to her and tell her to calm down
b. Keep out of her way
c. Say 'there, there' and try to pat her on the head

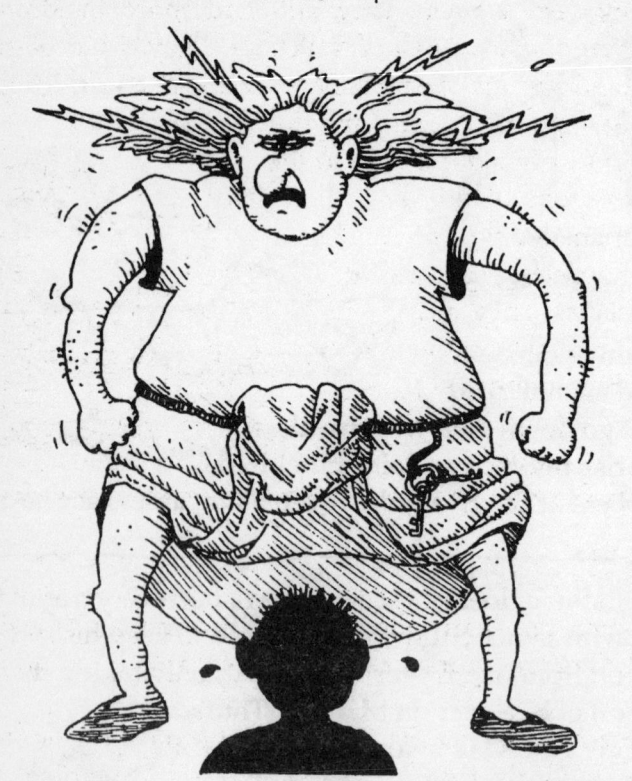

Answer on page 121

WOMEN'S WORK

Of course most women never became nuns and never lived in monasteries. If they hadn't got married and had children the Saxons would have died out and we wouldn't be speaking English today! In fact most English people wouldn't exist at all.

Although the position of Saxon women was nothing like as equal to men as the position of modern women, they still had more freedom than most women of that time. They could own land and make oaths of accusation in court. Also, women ruled inside the home. They carried the keys to the household and managed any household servants or slaves. They were especially famous for their embroidery, which was the best in all Europe.

PROFS IN PAIRS

Women ran many monasteries, but monks probably outnumbered nuns.

Most monasteries had schools: the oldest school in England is the King's School in Canterbury, which was started by Augustine. Boys as young as three went to live in monasteries, according to Bede, so that the monastic schools could teach them to read and write. Soon Saxon scholars were among the most learned in Northern Europe. Saxon missionaries, including many women, started to travel to the continent of Europe instead of the other way around.

Most of these English missionaries were Northumbrians. Take the two *Willies*:

Willibrord converted savage pagans back in Frisia, where the Saxons had come from in the first place.

Willibald became a bishop in Germany, then travelled even further, to Rome and then on to Syria and lands controlled by the Muslims.

> Missionary work could be dangerous. In 754 Saint Boniface, an English missionary to Frisia was massacred by a pagan band while quietly reading in his tent, along with fifty followers. Many of his fellow missionaries were probably women.

Back home the two bold *Alds* had a big impact:

Aldfrith was a son of Oswy. He was the first Saxon king to be more of a scholar than a warrior. Under his rule, Northumbria became a major centre of learning.

Aldhelm was a friend of Aldfrith. He was incredibly clever - so clever that practically no one can understand his writing! He liked to use as many difficult old-fashioned words as possible.

And we have to mention the two brilliant *Bs*:

Benedict Biscop collected books from all over Europe. He built up a big library in Jarrow near Wearmouth. In the Dark Ages books were more precious than gold.

Bede (Venerable) we've met before. He used Biscop's library to write his history of the Angles and Saxons.

Finally (he's not a pair of scholars, but he was worth a pair), there was *Alcuin*. Alcuin was one of Willibrord's relations. He started out as a humble scholar at York but ended up as a chief advisor to the Emperor Charlemagne in Europe.

The descendants of pagan warriors had become the favourite scholars of kings and emperors. Their monasteries were wealthy and paid no taxes.

It was all too good to be true ...

STRIKING VIKINGS

OH NO! THE BARBARIANS ARE BACK!

BEEN THERE, DONE THAT

In AD 793 a band of pagan raiders appeared out of the blue off the coast of Northumbria. They landed on the holy island of Lindisfarne and ransacked its monastery, the same monastery that had been founded by the Celtic Bishop Aidan over a hundred and fifty years before.

LOADSA LOOT!

The raiders came in three open boats, about thirty warriors to a boat ...
... remind you of anyone?

The raid on Lindisfarne in 793 was the first Viking attack on England. It took place more than three hundred years after the first Saxons raids on Britain, and the Saxons were completely unprepared for it. But if Hengist or Horsa or any other of the early Saxons had come back from the grave to watch those first Viking raiders, they might well have joined in!

Pagan Vikings and pagan Saxons were as alike as peas in the pod, even though the Viking attacks took place many years after those of the Saxons.

THE WORLD OF WODEN

- They both came from Northern Europe, although the Vikings came from a little further north, in Scandinavia.

- They both believed in the same gods. What the Saxons had called *Woden*, the Vikings called *Odin*, and what the Saxons had called *Thunor*, the Vikings called *Thor*. Odin of the Vikings still gathered the souls of warriors slain in battle, and Thor was still the god of thunder.

Considering how the Saxons had behaved when they first came to England, they scarcely had a leg to stand on. But they complained bitterly about the Vikings. As Bishop Alcuin put it:

'Lo, it is nearly 350 years that we and our fathers have inhabited this most lovely land and never before has such a terror appeared in Britain as we have now suffered from this pagan race.'

Above all both pagan Saxons and pagan Vikings loved war. When Viking warriors feasted in the halls of their chiefs, their shields and swords were hung up behind them, ready for battle at a moment's notice - just like the Saxon warriors of long ago.

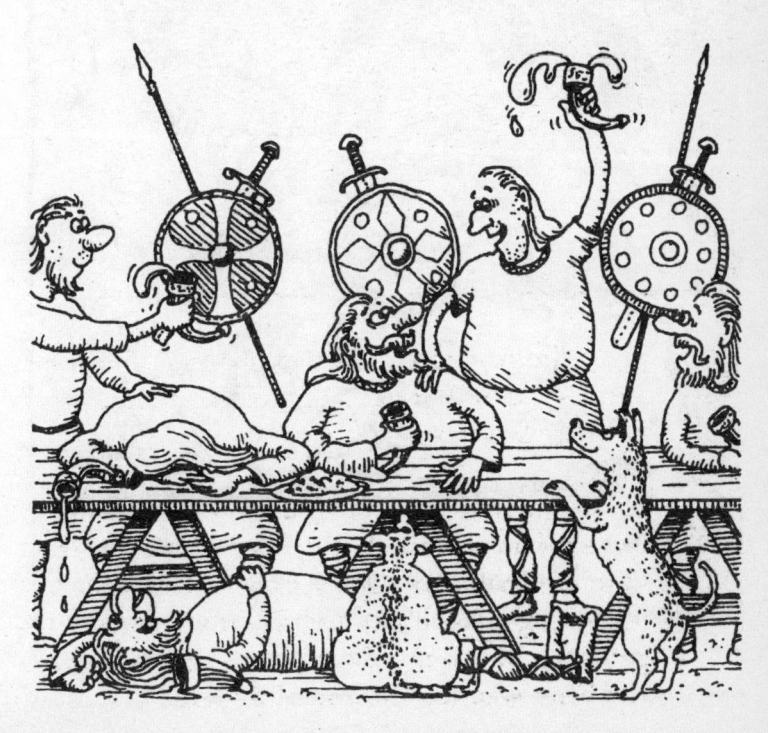

VICIOUS VIKINGS V. SURLY SAXONS

Who were more ruthless – pagan Saxons or pagan Vikings?

Answer

The early Saxons may have been even more ruthless than the Vikings. They seem to have gone in for more human sacrifice for instance. But no one really knows.

GRAB IT AND SCARPER

Vikings were to Saxons what a wasp is to a jammy finger, and what Saxons once were to Britons: they could move in quickly, cause maximum pain, and then buzz off before getting swatted. In other words: they came by sea, they struck where they wanted to, and then, while the poor old Saxons were getting ready to fight back, the Vikings would scarper with the loot.

Also, Viking ships were better than Saxon ships and Vikings were even better sailors. Their ships had sails but were still shallow enough to row far inland up rivers. Nowhere was safe in a narrow country with a long coastline like England.

Nowhere was safe, but monasteries were the least safe of all. There was loads of loot in Saxon monasteries and monks were men of peace who didn't carry weapons. Monasteries were easy pickings and Vikings went for them - like wasps for jam!

Even if a monastery or town wasn't near water, it might still be in danger of a Viking hit and run attack. Unlike the early Saxons, the Vikings made good use of horses. Sometimes they brought them with them and sometimes they rustled them on arrival. Either way, Viking war bands could travel almost as fast overland as they did by water, although they always dismounted before an attack and fought their battles on foot.

THE FIRST STOP-OVER

The early Viking raids were made by small bands of Norwegian Vikings who took what they could then cleared off back to Norway. The Saxon thegns had some success in fighting them off. They built defensive bridges across rivers - and they buried their money. Several treasure hoards of this period have been dug up, buried by Saxons in times of danger so that the Vikings couldn't get their hands on them. Too bad their owners were often killed before they could dig them up again!

As years went by the Viking raids grew bigger and the Danish Vikings joined in. In AD 850 a force of 350 ships stormed London and then Canterbury. They then decided to stop over for the winter to count their money - and to get ready for the following year. They made their winter camp on the Isle of Thanet in Kent.

This was the start of a new type of Viking warfare.

COME ON OVER!

Now Saxon England was on its knees and there was no time to recover before the fighting season started again in the spring. In 865 a 'great heathen host' led by three ruthless chiefs, Ubbe, Halfdan and Ivar the Boneless defeated King Ella of Northumbria and threw him into a pit where he was bitten to death by snakes. There was now a Viking kingdom in the north of England with its capital city at York.

England, let's face it, is a much nicer country than either Norway or Denmark. Among other things, the climate is warmer and the land is more fertile. The Vikings realized that they were on to a good thing.

Behind the Viking armies which ravaged eastern and northern England in the late 800s came another army - of settlers.

As with Saxon settlers of earlier times, it seems that the Vikings did not throw out all the farmers who were already working the land. Instead they set up new farms between the Saxon villages. The Viking settlers soon learned to speak English and before long it would be impossible to tell a Viking from a Saxon, just as it was impossible to tell an English Celt from a Saxon.

But that was for the future ...

OUR ALFRED

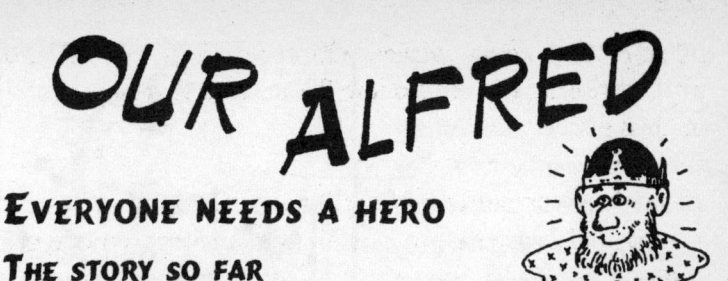

EVERYONE NEEDS A HERO
THE STORY SO FAR

LOADSA LOOT

LOADS MORE LOOT

SLAVES

AD 870 The 'Great Heathen Host' of the Vikings has moved south to Reading in the Saxon kingdom of Wessex, plundering and looting as it goes.

Aethelred King of Wessex and his younger brother Alfred lead their army against the Vikings in a series of battles, but fail to drive them from the kingdom.

AD 871 Aethelred dies and Alfred is chosen to be his successor. Alfred is just twenty-two or twenty-three years old. He will become the only English king ever to be called Great.

The Viking army moves north into the kingdom of Mercia then settles down for the winter in London.

The Vikings have become an experienced army and the Saxons are powerless against them. For the next seven years Vikings ravage the land like a swarm of locusts.

MAGNIFICENT MERCIANS

The kingdom of the *Mierce* or 'Boundary Folk' spread like a great big blob across the middle of England. Soon it would join with Wessex under Alfred's leadership to make an even bigger blob.

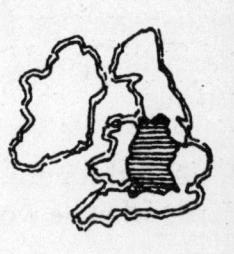

Mercian kings were descended from an ancient German over-king — 'the best of all mankind between the seas' who must have ruled both Angles and Saxons before they sailed to Britain. For this reason the Mercian royal family seems to have been more 'royal' than other Saxon royal families.

Magnificent Mercian No. 1 Under *Penda the Pagan* (577? - 655), Mercia became the most powerful kingdom in England.

Magnificent Mercian No. 2 Around 774 Offa became the most powerful king in England. He is famous for building *Offa's Dyke*, an earthwork which stretches for about a hundred kilometres right up the border between England and Wales. It was meant to keep out the Welsh.

This ancient king was called *Offa*. The later Mercian king Offa was probably named after him.

Back to Alfred

Half of Mercia had been totally ravaged by the great Viking army in 878. It became a Viking province. Meanwhile young Alfred had to hide in the Somerset marshes.

But Alfred fought back against the Vikings and won. Here's what he won:

- Guthrum, leader of the Viking army, was forced to convert to Christianity. Alfred was his godfather.

- The Vikings agreed to stay within the boundaries of 'Danelaw', the land under their control in the east of England.

- The Mercians accepted Alfred's leadership. In fact all English people not ruled by the Vikings submitted to him. They submitted willingly because they saw that Alfred was the best person to lead them against their common Viking enemy. England was starting to become a single country.

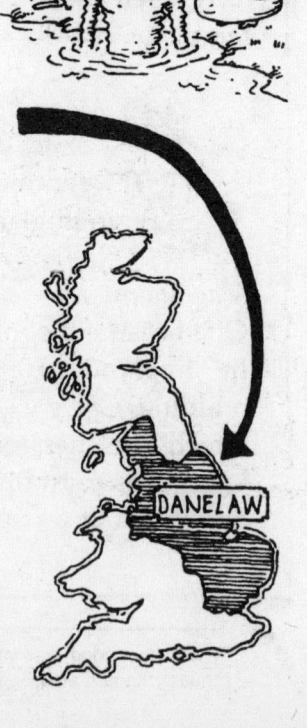

GREAT NEWS!

Take a look at these cuttings from the Saxon Klaxon and find out why Alfred was called 'great'.

MONSTER SHIPS!

Alfred has built the first English navy. His ships are larger than Viking ships and are expected to slaughter them if they get the chance.

BURGH BUILDING RECORDS SMASHED!

Walled towns or 'burghs' are being built at record rate. It is planned that no one in the kingdom will be more than fifteen kilometres from their nearest 'burgh' for refuge in case of attack by Viking marauders. Town walls are to be manned by one man from each hide of country round about and that should mean about one man every five metres of wall.

THEGNS TO SCHOOL!

Alfred has decreed that all his top noblemen must learn to read and write English. He hopes that in time all free Englishmen will be able to read.

ANGLO-SAXON CHRONICLE STARTED

Alfred has ordered the history of the Saxons to be written down in English, under the control of his Welsh friend, Bishop Asser.

The names of many of these towns, such as *Shrewsbury*, end in 'bury'.

ARMY SPLIT IN HALF!

The two halves of our army are to take it in turns to fight or to stay at home and do the farming. In this way it is reckoned that our forces will always be ready to fight off the Vikings and the crops will still be harvested - without our soldiers slinking off home in the middle of a war.

FORBIDDEN BRACELETS

Alfred has ordered golden bracelets be hung at some crossroads as a proof of the peace in his land and to show that in all his kingdom no one will steal them.

BAD MONK, GOOD MONK

Alfred was not just a mighty war leader. He had twice been taken to Rome when he was a child and had seen what civilization could be like at that time. He longed to be able to read books and write them. He asked a Saxon monk called John to help him reintroduce scholarship to England, but John was so severe in his religious beliefs that his fellow monks nearly killed him. John had to go.

Next Alfred asked the Welsh scholar Asser to come and help him. Asser didn't want to leave Wales and live among Saxons, but he agreed to come if he was allowed to spend six months of each year back home. Asser and Alfred soon became good friends and Asser taught Alfred to read and write Latin.

THREE STRONG KINGS

Alfred, his son *Edward* and his grandson *Athelstan* were three of the most powerful Saxon kings that ever ruled in England.

First the sad news: Alfred died in 899. All English people mourned.

Then the glad news: Alfred's successors kept up his good work. His son Edward was recognized as over-king by most of the rulers in Britain, and by 927 Athelstan, his grandson, had captured the Viking city of York.

> For the first time the England of both Vikings and Saxons was united under a single ruler. It was during this time that the system of 'shire' counties was started. It looked like England was in for a golden age.

> FAT HOPE!

SAXONS STUFFED!

ALL GOOD THINGS COME TO AN END

TO START WITH - A REALLY BAD KING

Aethelred the Unready (978 - 1016) ruled England for nearly forty disastrous years, and during that time he ruined most of the things Alfred had built up.

It started with a murder. In 978 Aethelred's half-brother was murdered by Aethelred's followers. Aethelred was too young to be blamed for the murder, but it was a bad beginning to his reign.

It went on to a massacre. Vikings could smell weakness. They soon knew that Aethelred was a feeble king and they started raiding again. By 1002 they had been at it for twenty years. In desperation and anger Aethelred ordered the

---

The name 'Aethelred the Unready' was originally 'Aethelred Unraed', meaning 'Aethelred No-council' or 'badly-advised'.

killing of all Danes ◄ then living in England. The sister of King Swein Forkbeard of Denmark was in England at the time. They killed her too - which wasn't very clever.

It continued with a mistake.
Aethelred married as his second wife Emma, sister of Duke Richard of Normandy (more on that later).

And it ended with a disaster.
In 1009 an army of King Swein Forkbeard of Denmark conquered England, partly to revenge the death of his sister. Aethelred fled abroad and the rest of his life was spent in desperate attempts to recover his kingdom.

THE PRICE OF PEACE ...

When Aethelred came to the throne, England was a wealthy nation. English coins were the best in Europe.

penig (penny)   sceat   styca

Dane was what the English called Vikings at this time.

The Vikings came to realize that they didn't need to bother with looting and pillaging. All they had to do was threaten it. Then, if they were lucky the Saxons would pay them to go away!

SAXON HOVEL

3,000 SCEATS OR IT BURNS!

The first payment of *Danegeld* as it was called was made in 868. Surprise, surprise, it had the opposite effect to what was intended - the Vikings came back for more - and more - and more. For the Vikings, Danegeld was like pocket money with no limits on it.

Strong kings like Alfred refused to pay it, but weak kings such as Aethelred saw Danegeld as an easy way to avoid trouble. Aethlered paid out massive sums of money to the Danes. They bled the country dry. More Saxon coins have been found in Scandinavia than have been found in England.

DANEFUL PAINS - AND NOT SO PAINFUL DANES

The Danes had been a pain for years. Looting and pillaging is not a way to get yourself liked. But they became Christians. And once Swein Forkbeard had defeated Aethelred, they were kings of all England - and things started to change.

1. Swein Forkbeard - a bit of a Viking

2. Swein's son Cnut - a good king. The English liked him.

3. Harthacnut - Cnut's son, both good and bad

Harthacnut died while drinking in 1041. He was the last of the three Danish kings of England. After his death Edward (later known as 'The Confessor') was chosen to be king. Edward's stepfather had been King Cnut, but Edward was a Saxon - his real father was Aethelred the Unready. Anything to do with Aethelred was bad news for England - and Edward was really no exception.

Normal Normans

In 911 a huge Viking called Rollo 🦶 knelt to kiss the foot of Charles the Simple, King of France, as an act of homage. The king had just given him lands in what is now Normandy as part of a peace treaty. Except that Rollo didn't kneel, he pulled the king's foot up to his mouth thus making the king fall over backwards. How Rollo's Viking friends laughed - typical!

Despite his rude behaviour Rollo became the first Duke of Normandy, and that's why Normandy is called what it is, after the 'nor(th)men' who were given it. The Normans started off as bullies, and that's how they stayed - as the Saxons were soon to discover ...

And grumpy Saxons

Edward the Confessor liked Normans. He spent his youth in Normandy because his mother Emma was a Norman, and he filled his court in London with Norman friends after he came to the throne.

Possibly the same person as a Viking known as *Hrolf the Ganger*, or 'Walker', so called because he was so big no horse could carry him.

In 1052 the Duke of Normandy himself, a red-haired man called William, visited Edward the Confessor in London. It seems that during this visit Edward promised the crown of England to William - and changed the course of English history.

Edward invited more and more Normans to join him in England. It seemed to many Saxons that the Normans were taking over. The Saxon lords became fed up and grumpy. The grumpiest were led by a powerful earl called Harold Godwine.

Then on 5 January 1066 Edward died. His council were in an anti-French mood. They decided Harold Godwine was the right man to be the next king of England.

William Duke of Normandy did not agree ...

THE END

Harold scarcely had time to slip the crown of England on his head. By September he was being squeezed in the middle of a horrible sandwich. To the north, an army of Norwegian Vikings had already landed. To the south, an army of Normans led by William the Duke was just about to land.

Harold rushed north and defeated the Norwegians at a place called Stamford Bridge. Then he rushed south again to beat off the Normans, who were waiting for him at Hastings in Sussex. William's Norman army was smaller than Harold's, but they hadn't just fought an army of Norwegians and they hadn't just marched south at top speed for three hundred kilometres. The Normans were ready for a fight, but the Saxons could have done with a rest.

The Saxon and Norman armies met on the morning of 14 October on the road to Hastings. Not so very far from the beach in Kent where Hengist and Horsa had landed in AD 449 all that long time ago. To start with, the two-handed Saxon battleaxes sliced through the armour of the Norman knights, but slowly the Normans gained the upper hand. Harold and his companions fought bravely all day, but finally Harold was killed by a chance Norman arrow and Saxon resistance started to crumble.

In fact the Saxon shield-wall held firm till almost the end. Every time a warrior fell the other warriors drew closer to cover the space where the fallen man had stood, until the shield-wall was little more than a ragged line.

Saxon England came to an end that day, but Hengist and Horsa, those fierce warriors, would have been proud of the warriors who fought and died at Hastings.

ARE YOU AN ANGLE OR A SAXON?

– OR A NORMAN OR A CELT?

SAXONS SUMMED UP

William Duke of Normandy, soon to be known as 'William the Conqueror', lost no time in seizing control of the rest of England. Within a few years the whole of Saxon England was being ruled by Frenchmen, and the Saxon Age had come to an end. The Middle Ages was about to begin.

But life goes on. William had won a rich prize and he had no wish to disturb or destroy it. He chose to rule by the laws and customs of the Saxons. Because of this we owe far more to the Saxons than we do to the Normans who defeated them.

> **THINGS WE HAVE INHERITED FROM THE SAXONS**
>
> the words 'England' and 'English'
> the English language
> the days of the week
> the English system of law
> most English towns and villages
> most English counties
> – in fact almost everything English

Throughout history waves of newcomers have arrived on the islands of Britain. There was a time when the Celts were new, even before the Saxons came along. Each new wave of newcomers has mixed and mingled with the people who were there when they arrived.

> The Saxons weren't the first newcomers, and they certainly weren't the last, but they changed Britain more than any other group of people before or after them.

BYE FOR NOW!

SAINTED!

So maybe you're the right type to be a savage Saxon - but could you have been a glad-to-be-good Saxon (or even a saint)? Let's find out - part 2.

1. DO YOU LIKE SMELLY FEET?

a. Not really, but not washing is a good way for a saint to behave
b. They smell disgusting
c. They smell nice - but saints aren't meant to enjoy themselves

2. WHAT'S GOOD ABOUT DOUBLE MONASTERIES?

a. You have to say twice the prayers of a single monastery
b. You get to meet lots of nice monks or nuns of the opposite sex
c. Double monasteries are all right as long as you never meet the opposite sex

3. WHAT'S GOOD ABOUT BEING A SAINT?

a. You go to heaven when you die
b. Nothing - it's really boring
c. You never have to wash and you get to meet lots of interesting people

(Answers on next page)

What kind of a Saxon would you have been?
Answers

Section 1

Are you the right type to be as seriously savage Saxon?
Score 10 points for each correct answer.

Part 1	Part 2	Part 3	Part 4
1 - c	1 - a	1 - c	a
2 - c	2 - c	2 - b	
3 - a	3 - b	3 - a	

Section 2

Could you have been a glad-to-be-good Saxon (or even a Saxon saint)?
Score *minus* 10 points for each correct answer.

Part 1	Part 2
1 - b	1 - a
2 - a	2 - c
3 - b	3 - a or b

Grand Total

To arrive at your final total, **subtract** points scored in section 2 from points scored in section 1.

- **60 to 100** — You are seriously savage. Got any long, sharp knives?
- **30 to 60** — Not bad - for a churl. You'll be all right on a war party.
- **0 to 30** — What a wimp! Go back to noddy-land!
- **-30 to 0** — You are seriously good.
- **-30 to -60** — You are disgustingly good - and you stink like a ferret!

Index

Adomnan 23
Aethelberht 70
Aethelfrith the Ferocious, 32, 71
Aethelred (King of Wessex) 103-4
Aethelred the Unready 110-113
Aidan 79, 95
Alcuin 94, 97
Aldfrith 93
Aldhelm 93
Alfred the Great 47-8, 103-10, 112
Ambrosius Aurelianus 31
Anderida 19
Aneirin 32
Angels 69
Angles 6-7, 13, 28, 35, 38, 69-70, 93, 105
Anglo-Saxon Chronicle 9, 11, 107
Armour 21-2
Arthur, King 31-4
Asser 107-8
Athelstan 21, 109
Augustine 69-70, 77-8, 83, 91

Barbarians 6, 12, 15-16, 18, 95
Bath 34
Bathing 59, 89
Battleaxes 117
Bede 9, 91, 93
Beowulf 9, 43
Bernicia 35
Bible 77
Biscop, Benedict 93
Boats, 7, 21, 95
Bone-fights 12, 42
Boniface 92
Bran 33
Brendan 78
Bretwaldas 36, 38, 80
Britons 16-19, 29, 29-31, 33-4, 77-8, 99
Brittany 29
Brythonic 12, 14
Burghs 108

Caedbad 27
Caedwalla 75-6
Canterbury 70, 91, 101
Cantii 18
Caroles 45
Catterick 32
Celts 14-15, 27, 77, 79, 83, 102, 119
Cerdic 26-8
Charlemagne 94
Charles the Simple 114
Chester, Battle of 71
Churls 46-8, 54, 57, 63
Clothing 10, 21-2, 89
Cnut 113
Coifi 74
Coins 111-12
Cornwall 77

Coronations 36
Cottar 57-8
Craftsmen 38
Cuthbert 89
Cymry 26

Danegeld 112
Danelaw 106
Danes 111-13
Days of the week 67, 118
Deira 35
Din Eidyn 32
Dragons 68
Drinking horns 8, 42
Duelling 50, 52
Dumnonia 30
Durham 85

Ealdormen 53-4
East Anglia 28, 35, 73
Easter 66, 80, 82-3, 86, 88-9
Edgar 60
Edward 109
Edward the Confessor 113-15
Edwin 73-5, 79-80
Ella 101
Elmet 30
Elves 58, 67
Embroidery 91
Emma of Normandy 111, 114
English 12-13, 27, 91, 102, 107, 118
Eostre 66
Essex 35
Etheldreda 89

Fates 61
Feasts 5, 40-2
Food 59-60

Fountains 30
Franks 37
Fransisca 21
Frig 67
Frisia 92
Frisians 7

Geats 43
Germanus 29
Gesith 39, 46
Giants 55, 67
Gildas 9
Goddodin 30, 32
Gods 16, 22, 33, 37, 62-7, 73, 76, 96
Great Heathen Host 101, 103
Gregory I 69-70, 72
Grendel 43
Guthrum 106
Gwyned 30

Haethfield, Battle of 75
Halfdan, 101
Halls 5, 39-41, 43, 56, 73, 97
Ham 25
Harold Godwine 115-17
Harthacnut 113
Hastings, Battle of 116-17
Hengist 18-19, 31, 96, 116-17
Hides 47-8, 54
Hilda 88
Horsa 18-19, 31, 96, 116-17
Hundreds 48, 53
Huts 55-6

Illness 58-9

123

Iona 78-80
Ireland 14-15, 77
Ivar the Boneless 101

Jarrow 93
Jutes 7, 35

Kent 18-19, 31, 35, 29, 70, 73, 101
King lists 9
Kings, Saxon 9, 26-7, 29, 36-9, 45-7, 93
King's School 91

Laws 12, 20, 23, 48, 52, 60, 118
Lindisfarne 79-80, 95
Lindsey 27, 35

Maldon, Battle of 39
Mercia 35-6, 104-6
Middlesex 35
Missionaries 71-3, 77, 79, 87, 92
Monasteries 79-80 86-8, 91, 94-5, 99-100, 120
Monks 23, 33, 69-70, 78-80, 86, 88-9, 91, 99, 108
Months 64-5
Moot 48
Mount Badon, Battle of 33-4

Nennius 9, 33
Normandy 114, 118
Normans 36, 114-118
Northumbria 29, 35-7, 73, 75-6 79, 81, 93, 95, 101
Nuns 88-9, 91

Odin 96
Offa 21, 23, 105
Offa's Dyke 105
Open-field system 57
Oswald 79-82, 84-5
Oswestry 80, 84
Oswy 36, 81-4, 93

Parchment 8, 31
Paulinus 73-4
Peada 85
Penda 75-6, 80, 84-5, 105
Penig 111
Picts 15, 30
Pirates 7, 15, 29
Powys 30
Punishment 51, 52, 58

Raedwald 38, 72
Reeves 53
Richard of Normandy 111
Rollo 114
Roman Empire 8, 14, 16, 77
Romano-Britons 14, 18, 55

Sacrifices 63, 73, 98
Saturn 67
Saxnot 37
Saxon Shore 15
Saxony 34
Scalping 51
Sceaf 7
Sceats 111-12
Schools 91-2, 107
Scotland 14-15, 32-3, 77-8
Scots 15, 18
Scramasaxe 21
Sherrifs 53-4
Shield wall 23, 117

Shillings 47
Ships, Saxon 20, 38, 99, 107
Ships, Viking 99, 101, 107
Shires 53-4
Slaves 46, 57-8, 103
Stamford Bridge, Battle of 116
Styca 111
Sussex 19, 35, 116
Sutton Hoo 38, 73
Swein Forkbeard 111, 113

Tacitus 10, 22, 39, 55, 88
Terpens 7
Thegns 39, 46-8, 54, 57, 72-4, 100, 107
Thor 63, 96
Thunor 22, 63, 67, 96
Tiw 67
Tonsures 83, 86
Treasure hoards 38, 100
Triads 9
Tribute 57

Ubbe 101

Vikings 39, 62-3, 95-104, 106-114, 116
Vortigern 18-19, 31

Wales 14, 75, 77, 105, 108
Wappentakes 37
Wergild 46-8, 51, 52
Wessex 26, 28, 35-6, 46-7, 103, 105
Whitby, Synod of 83, 86, 88
Wilfred 83-4
William the Conquerer, 115-16, 118
Willibald 92

Willibrord 92, 94
Witans 41, 54
Woad 15
Woden 37, 62-3, 67, 73-4, 96
Women 23, 41, 50, 87-8, 90-2

York 75, 94, 101, 109

Now Read On

If you want to know more about the Romans in Britain, see if your local library or bookshop has any of these books.

The warrior kings of Saxon England
By Ralph Whitlock (Moonraker Press 1977) If you like a good fight, then this is the book for you! All you need to know about the brave heroes who led the Saxon fight against the Vikings.

Northanhymbre Saga
By John Marsden (Kyle Cathie Ltd. 1992) Delve into a depth of detail about the Dark Ages. An excellent introduction to Aethelfrith the Ferocious, Penda the Last of the Pagans and their bloodthirsty mates.

Alfred the Great
By Ronald Mcnair Scott (The Book Guild Ltd. 1993) Follow the story of England's greatest king from his birth in war-torn Wessex and his time on the run in the Somerset marshes, to his great victories and his friendship with Asser the reluctant Welsh bishop.

The Anglo-Saxons
Edited by James Campbell (Phaidon Press Ltd. 1982) More photographs than you could fit on your bedroom wall! - well almost. Get behind the words (there's lots of them as well) and take a look at the evidence. If you remember half of what's in this book, you'll be an expert on the Saxons.

What they don't tell you about

VIKINGS

By Bob Fowke

Dedicated to Egil Skallagrimsson,
a writer who knew how to handle a sword.

Hodder Children's Books

A division of Hodder Headline Limited

> Hallo, my name's *Bjorn the Blood-Crazy*. Pay attention or I'll slice your head from your shoulders with one blow of my trusty battleaxe. You're about to join me and my *venomous* Viking pals on a really *bloody* adventure. So get ready, I'll make sure you *bite into* all the really *gory* bits.

What They Don't Tell You About Vikings first published as a single volume in Great Britain in 1996 by Hodder Children's Books.

Text and illustrations copyright © Bob Fowke 1996

WHAT'S IN THIS BOOK

SMASH AND GRAB!
THEY CAME, THEY SAW, THEY TOOK
Page 5

WHO DUNNIT?
INTRODUCING MR AND MRS VIKING
Page 9

HOME SWEET HOME
WE'RE JUST FARMERS!
Page 20

WILD WOMEN
- SO WATCH OUT!
Page 29

HAIRY KINGS, BALD SLAVES AND ER ... THING
WHO'S ON TOP - AND WHO ISN'T
Page 36

DRUNK AS A SCANDINAVIAN SKUNK
TIME FOR BEER AND BALLADS
Page 46

WAR FEVER!
SUMMER HOLIDAYS VIKING-STYLE
Page 51

ROW, ROW, ROW THE BOAT
A FIGHT ON THE OCEAN WAVE
Page 61

Watch out for the *Sign of the Foot*! Whenever you see this sign in the book it means there are some more details at the *FOOT* of the page. Like here.

Go West, Young Man
But first you have to know the way
Page 68

All Right Then, Go East!
Raiders in river boats
Page 79

The Bulldog Bites Back
Britain at battle-stations
– the story so far
Page 90

Disaster Strikes Again!
Page 97
England – the story so far

Drunk For Ever!
Page 106
– well, not quite

What Happened Next?
Page 117
Turn christian – or else!

Years of Fear
A handful of dates
Page 121

Villainous Vikings Hall of Fame Page 123

Index Page 127

Keep your eyes open for the *Blood-splat Spot!* When the blood-splat splats beside a name this means there are more details in the *Villainous Vikings Hall of Fame* on page 123.

> First of all, let's find out how everything started.

SMASH AND GRAB!

THEY CAME, THEY SAW, THEY TOOK

It's early morning on the 8th June AD 793. A tired grumpy monk wipes his bleary eyes - never a decent night's sleep when you have to go to church in the middle of every night. And this year his sleep has been ruined by freak whirlwinds and extra powerful lightning. There has even been talk of dragons flying in the air, although he hasn't seen any.

And now it's time for church again.

He glances out of the narrow window of his tiny cell. The sea looks grey and wild beneath a stormy sky. His monastery is Saint Aidan's

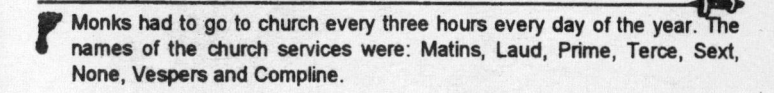

Monks had to go to church every three hours every day of the year. The names of the church services were: Matins, Laud, Prime, Terce, Sext, None, Vespers and Compline.

of Lindisfarne, a small island known as Holy Island, off the coast of Northumberland. All traffic between the monastery and the mainland is by a four-kilometre causeway which is underwater at high tide.

Lindisfarne is not an easy place to run away from.

Gazing wistfully out to sea, he sees some small dark specks bobbing far out on the water. Surely they can't be ships, there are too many of them? He looks more carefully; they're ships all right, and an unusual shape. They curve upwards at the ends and look like dragons' heads. He blinks. Oh no, now he's seeing dragons too - that's what lack of sleep can do to you.

That's almost the only warning that Western Europe got of the Vikings. They appeared out of the blue and fell on Lindisfarne on that June day in AD 793 like a pack of blood-crazed hyenas. Here's how the attack was described by another monk, called Simeon, who lived in Durham three hundred years later:

> (Aaargh!)
>
> ..the heathens from the northern regions came with a fleet of ships to Britain. They came to the church of Lindisfarne, laid everything waste with grievous plundering, trampled the holy places with polluted steps, dug up the altars and seized all the treasures of the holy church. They killed some of the monks, took some away with them in fetters, many they drove out naked and loaded with insults, some they drowned in the sea.

Heathen meant people who weren't Christian, Jewish or Muslim. It comes from '*heath-dwellers*' or wild people who lived on the heath.

Lindisfarne was the beginning of some of the bloodiest years in European history. Vikings found out that attacking monasteries was like ram-raiding without the risks. There was lots of treasure in monasteries and the monks weren't used to defending themselves.

But Vikings didn't stop at monasteries. The attack on Lindisfarne was the start of a reign of terror that went on for the next two hundred years ...

WHO DUNNIT?

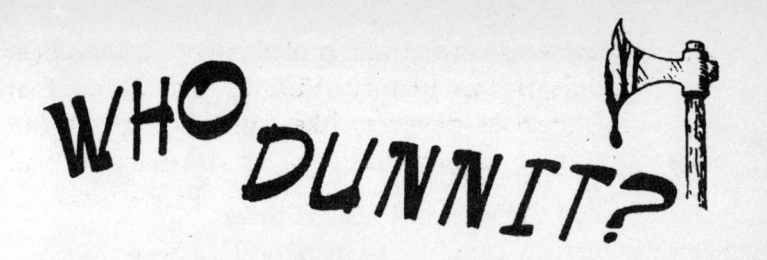

INTRODUCING MR AND MRS VIKING

When the raid was over, the raiders of Lindisfarne escaped out to sea with their slaves and booty and headed north across the wild North Sea. They came from what is now called Scandinavia.

THE VIKING AGE LASTED FROM AD 800 TO 1100

ARCTIC CIRCLE

NORWAY

SWEDEN

DENMARK

THIS WAY TO SANTA'S GROTTO

SCANDINAVIA IS MADE UP OF NORWAY, SWEDEN AND DENMARK

BRITAIN WAS SPECIALLY VULNERABLE TO VIKING ATTACK BECAUSE IT HAD SUCH A LONG COAST LINE.

SITE OF WHITEHART LANE FOOTBALL GROUND

LOVELY AND HOT DOWN HERE

We looked pretty good, though I say so myself.

HIM

People were scared stiff of Vikings, but they liked the look of these 'ruthless wrathful foreign purely pagan people' as one monk described them. This is what a Viking chief looked like in *Njall's Saga* 🐾 , written in Iceland:

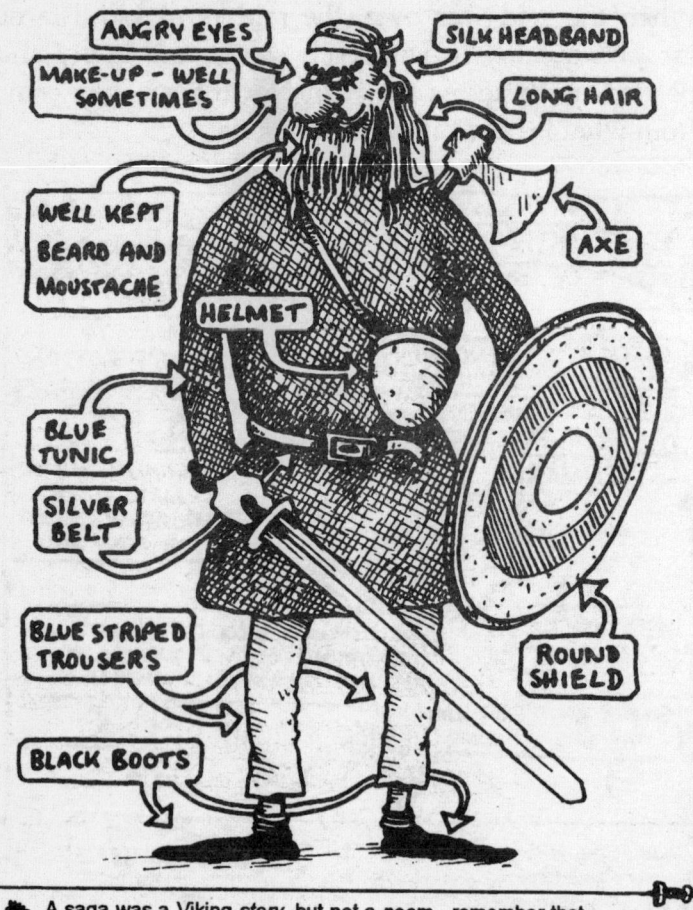

- ANGRY EYES
- SILK HEADBAND
- MAKE-UP – WELL SOMETIMES
- LONG HAIR
- WELL KEPT BEARD AND MOUSTACHE
- AXE
- HELMET
- BLUE TUNIC
- SILVER BELT
- BLUE STRIPED TROUSERS
- ROUND SHIELD
- BLACK BOOTS

🐾 A saga was a Viking *story*, but not a *poem* - remember that.

HER

Before they became Christian, pagan 🦶 Vikings could have more than one wife plus several concubines 🦶. Viking women were known for their independent ways. The top wife of a Viking was seen as almost the equal of her husband. She showed this by hanging her keys from a brooch on her chest.

- MARRIED WOMEN WORE A HEAD SCARF
- NECK RING
- BREAST BROOCHES
- KEYS
- SEWING TOOLS
- MITTENS IN WINTER
- LENGTHS OF EXPENSIVE CLOTH
- PLEATED LINEN PETTICOAT
- SOFT LEATHER SHOES

🦶 A pagan is like a heathen. In this book it means people who worshipped the old Viking gods.

🦶 Concubines were women who lived with a man but were not married.

A BIT OF BACKGROUND

The very first account of Scandinavia is by an ancient Greek called Pytheas who sailed from Marseilles in the south of France around 330 BC, looking for a sea route to the tin and amber trade of Northern Europe. He sailed up the coast of Norway to a land called Thule, where he found people who hunted for seals, whales, fish and seagulls.

Seagull

The people seen by Pytheas must have been the ancestors of the Vikings, known as the *Battle-Axe People*, who arrived in Scandinavia from the south around two thousand years earlier. The Battle-Axe People left pictures of themselves wearing horned helmets and fighting with axes.

The lifestyle of the Vikings was like the Battle-Axe people. They were mostly off-duty farmers who spent the rest of the year, when they weren't raiding, knee-

---

Their Viking descendants did not wear horns on their helmets. Horns are not very practical when fighting. They can catch a sword-blow and are easy to grab hold of.

deep in cow-muck or minding their sheep on the Scandinavian hillsides. Here's a typical farm:

THE GRABBIT HABIT

No one knows for sure why the Vikings got in the habit of raiding. Perhaps it was a mixture of reasons:

Be that as it may, they certainly liked ships - the word *Viking* seems to have come from an old word 'vik' meaning a bay or creek. In fact the Vikings usually described themselves by the area they came from ...

Other people called them Norsemen, Danes or Rus, as well as a lot of names which are too rude to print!

HOW DID THEY GET AWAY WITH IT?

The reason a bunch of off-duty farmers from a freezing cold land in the far north could smash up the rest of Europe was because Europe was going through a bad patch at the time ...

EUROPE IN AD 814

VIKINGS COULD RAID FAR INLAND UP RIVERS

EMPEROR CHARLEMAGNE DIED IN 814. HIS EMPIRE DIVIDED.

HUNS INVADED EUROPE FROM THE EAST ON HORSEBACK.

SARACENS, OR ARABS, INVADED FROM THE SOUTH.

The Huns later settled down in what is now Hungary.

14

MONK STORY

As the monks of Lindisfarne had found out, it was a specially bad time to be a monk because monasteries were full of treasure. Take the monks of St. Philibert, in France:

600 Monastery on the island of Noirmoutier on the river Loire.

862 Monks move inland to Poitou to escape Viking raids.

872-3 Monks move further inland to Moulins.

875 They move to Tournus, still trying to escape Viking raids; they had fled 965 km in 13 years.

937 Raided again - by Huns from the east!

SEARCHING FOR CLUES

The Vikings lived at a time of war and barbarian invasion. Not many people were writing books so we don't know much about them. In fact so little remains that investigating them is like trying to solve some complicated puzzle with half the bits missing. Fortunately the Vikings left a handful of clues behind:

CLUE NO 1 - THE DAYS OF THE WEEK

The gods of the old English and the Vikings were very similar. Some of our weekdays are named after the same gods as the Viking gods. Viking gods were fierce and quarrelsome - like the people.

The sky god and god of war was called Tyr in Scandinavia and Tiw in England. Prisoners of war may have been sacrificed to him. Tuesday is named after him.

The top god was called Woden in England and Odin by the Vikings. Wednesday (Woden's Day) is his day. More about him later.

Thor was the god of thunder, among other things. He was a vast red-haired man with a red beard and red eyebrows. He carried a hammer called Mjolnir and had a pair of iron gauntlets. When he rode across the sky in his chariot drawn by two sacred goats the thunder rumbled and crashed. Thursday is named after him.

Frigg or Freyya was the goddess of love and the home. She had lots of arguments with her husband, Odin, which she often won. Friday is her day.

CLUE NO 2 - PLACE NAMES

Some Vikings stayed on after the raiding season was over. In several countries they settled in large numbers and mixed with the local people. We can tell where they settled by looking at the names of towns and villages. In north-west England there are hundreds of places ending in '-by', such as Weatherby; 'by' was Viking for a small village or farm.

CLUE NO 3 - BURIED TREASURE

A lot of clues about the Vikings have been found underground. Several rich 'hoards' have been found of objects beautifully made of gold, silver and iron. Archaeologists have also found out a lot about how the Vikings lived from everyday objects which may not be treasure but can be even more interesting.

CLUE NO No 4 - RUNES

The Vikings had their own alphabet called Runic. They carved messages on wayside stones and in other places such as bridges. Some historians can read the messages.

CLUE NO 5 - SAGAS AND POEMS

Sagas and poems were normally about exciting adventures, heroes and myths. Poems were remembered and spoken aloud at first. Later some of them were written down.

CLUE NO 6 - THE ANGLO-SAXON CHRONICLE

The Saxons lived in England during the Viking period. They kept a record of everything important which happened each year. The Anglo-Saxon Chronicle describes many Viking attacks (see page 94).

Archaeologists are historians who specialise in digging up remains from the past.

Could YOU Have Dunnit?

Check it out - are you bad Viking material? (part 1)

1 Which toy do you like best?

a A doll
b A blood-stained axe
c A model boat

2 Which is Right?

a Friday was once the traditional day for human sacrifice by frying the victims.
b Friday was once a free-day or holiday.
c Friday is named after a goddess called Frigg or Freyya.

3 Which game do you like best?

a Mummies and Daddies
b Fighting
c Football

(Answers on page 122.)

HOME SWEET HOME

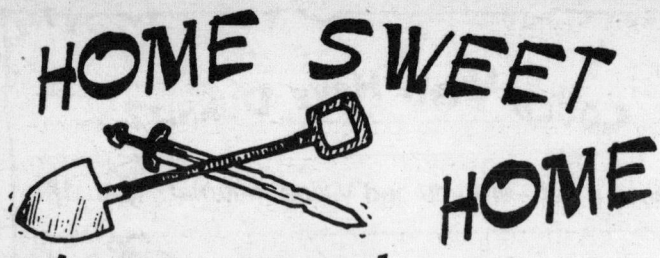

WE'RE JUST FARMERS!

Scandinavia is freezing cold for a lot of the year especially in the far north. The first Viking raiders of Britain probably came from Norway, where remote scattered farms still cling to the steep hills as they sweep down towards the icy fjords below. (In the south the farms were clustered together in villages). Life was tough for the small-time farmers who made up the backbone of Viking raiding parties.

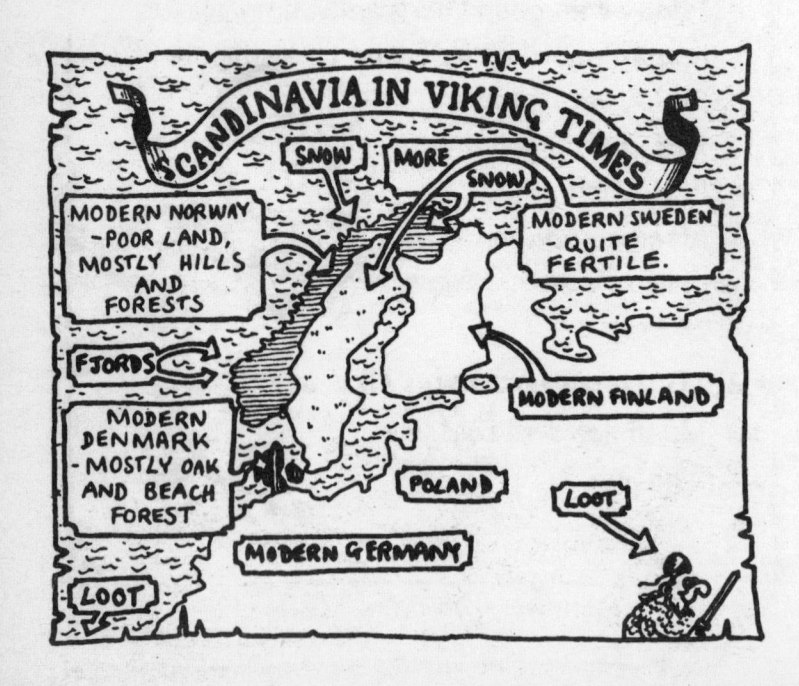

SCANDINAVIA IN VIKING TIMES

- SNOW
- MORE SNOW
- MODERN NORWAY – POOR LAND, MOSTLY HILLS AND FORESTS
- MODERN SWEDEN – QUITE FERTILE.
- FJORDS
- MODERN FINLAND
- MODERN DENMARK – MOSTLY OAK AND BEACH FOREST
- POLAND
- LOOT
- MODERN GERMANY
- LOOT

GETTING THERE

It was hard to travel from one farm to another on the muddy tracks and there were no bridges anywhere as far as we know. So winter, when the mud was frozen, was the easiest time to get around. When the snow came a Viking on the move would wrap up warm against the bitter cold before strapping on a pair of skis, skates or snow-shoes, all of which were invented by the ancestors of the Vikings.

Skis were good for sport as well as travel.

Skates were made of bone, and skaters would push themselves around on the ice with spoked sticks.

They also had sledges and would fit iron spikes onto horses' hooves so that they could get a better grip on the ice.

Home at Last!

At night in the far north the cold can freeze your eyeballs and worse 🔍, so the houses for both people and animals have to be extra warm. When they settled in Greenland near the Arctic Circle the Vikings built cowsheds like castles against the cold, with turf walls nearly two metres thick and with a great mound of turf piled on top for a roof. The entrances were long narrow passages to keep out as much cold air as possible.

A typical Viking liked his house to be long - very long. Usually there was one enormous room with walls which curved inwards at the ends, a reminder of earlier times when upturned boats were used as roofs. Their longhouses might be made out of wood or stones or even entirely out of turf like the Greenland cowsheds. In turf houses, dry wood panels were built inside, standing free of the damp turf walls.

People ate and slept on wide earth platforms which ran down both sides of a longhouse. The low rough gulley between them was used for cooking and for a fire, and probably for leaving muddy boots. There was no chimney; the stench of smoke, food, animals and unwashed bodies must have been enough to make a skunk vomit.

> When people suffer from frost-bite the frozen bits, usually fingers and toes but sometimes the nose and ears, go black and then fall off.

INSIDE A LONGHOUSE

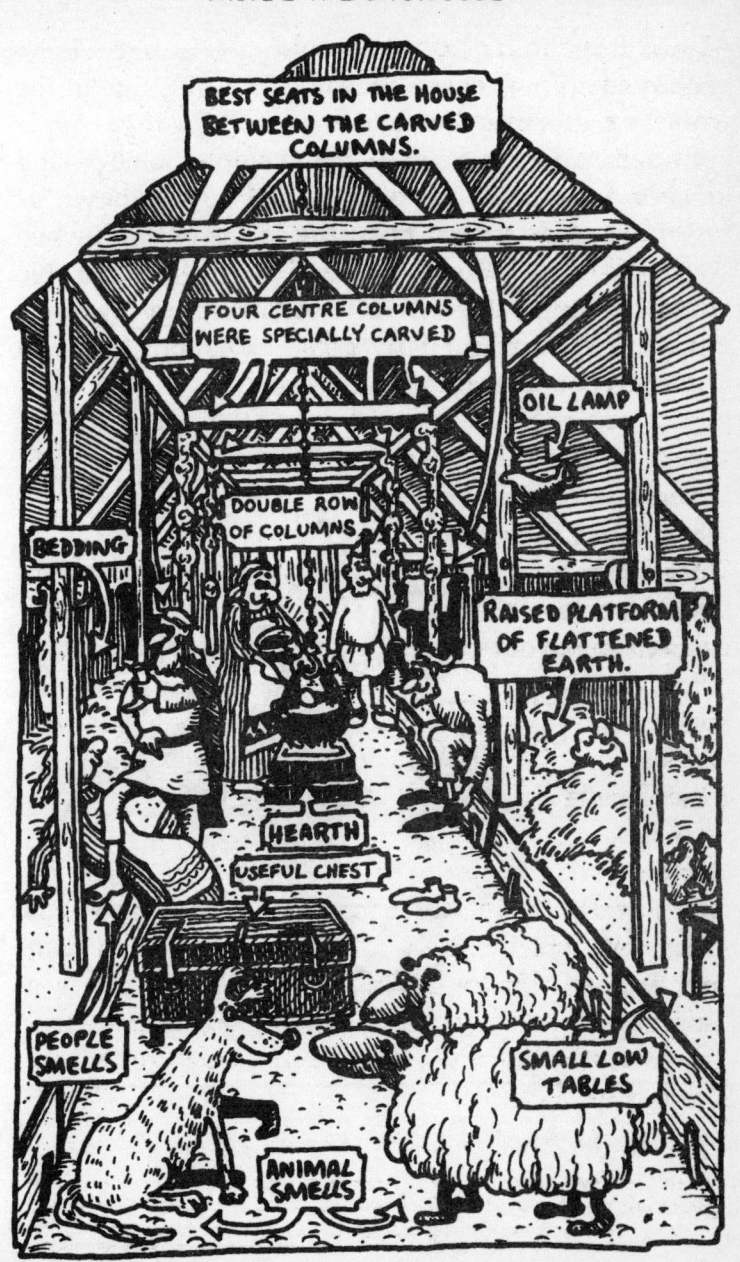

- BEST SEATS IN THE HOUSE BETWEEN THE CARVED COLUMNS.
- FOUR CENTRE COLUMNS WERE SPECIALLY CARVED
- OIL LAMP
- DOUBLE ROW OF COLUMNS
- BEDDING
- RAISED PLATFORM OF FLATTENED EARTH.
- HEARTH
- USEFUL CHEST
- PEOPLE SMELLS
- SMALL LOW TABLES
- ANIMAL SMELLS

GRUB'S UP

Apart from big feasts which were a favourite Viking hobby, there were two main meals a day, one in the morning after everyone had been working for a couple of hours, and the other in the evening. Some Viking dishes are still eaten today. Blood soup, known as *svartsoppa* was a great favourite in the autumn when the pigs were slaughtered and is still popular. No doubt Vikings ate an early version of *smorgasbord*, which meant 'smear fatty goose table' but is now a collection of cold meats and cheeses.

People slurped up their blood soup and other tasty morsels with spoons made out of wood or deer's antler. They used wooden bowls and flat wooden trenchers, which are like a sort of plate.

Vikings who settled in Iceland hardly ate any greens, just a few leeks and a bit of seaweed.

A Hunting We Will Go

Most Vikings liked to hunt. In the far north hunting was vital for survival.

TASTY MORSELS

Seagull eggs were very popular.

Seabirds were snared or shot with arrows.

FOR THAT EXTRA SOMETHING
Furs, hides, whalebone, walrus tusks, live falcons and feathers were all traded for luxuries from further south.

A SUBSTANTIAL MEAL
Bear, wild boar, elk and reindeer were all hunted and eaten. Seals were speared or netted, while whales were harpooned from small boats then towed ashore.

AH, DINNER!

> The farming life could be tough and boring. Raiding was much more fun.

DEAR DIARY
A Year in the Life of Harald Homebody

Six Winter Months
Stay indoors, too cold to go out apart from a little hunting and fighting. Shall get on with some indoor work, and if that's too boring, there's always feasting.

April (Cuckoo Month)
Time to put the boots on, must start ploughing. The slaves can do a bit of peat-digging and wood-cutting for next winter's fire. Oh, and they'll have to repair the walls round the fields and make sure they're well-manured with dung. My son, Thorkil, is due to set off on a raiding expedition this month. I don't think I'll go with him - still got a bit of trouble with the sword wound I collected in Northumbria last August.

May - June (Lambs'-Fold Time)
Must send the slaves and children to gather seabirds' eggs from the cliffs. I shall get on with the lamb-weaning and later the sheep-shearing. Also I must go and defend myself at the local *Thing* . Someone says that I killed their son last winter - well I was drunk and he called me a pig. What's wrong with being drunk?

Thing was the Viking word for an assembly. It was a cross between a local law court and a parliament.

June - July
Drive the cattle and sheep to the high pastures, the slaves can stay with them.

July - August (Hay-Making Month)
All hands to the scythe! Women and children as well as free men and slaves. Must collect as much hay as possible, not just from the fields, but from the open countryside. Then it's time to start harvesting the cereal crops such as oats and rye - I'm exhausted!

September - October
Round up the animals from the mountain pastures and sort them out by their ear-marks. Some must be slaughtered and the meat dried or salted to stop it going bad. Lots of lovely pig's blood to eat during the slaughter - yum!

Winter again
Must break down the walls round the cornfields so that the cattle can get to the stubble. Thorkil's back safe and sound and he's brought lots of treasure. Beginning of winter is a good time for feasts, as we've still got plenty of fresh food, and not too much work to do.

> The scruffy English said we had an unfair advantage with the local girls because we bathed once a week, combed our hair and changed our underwear.

SAVAGE SAUNAS

After a hard day's hunting or farming there was nothing a Viking liked better than a good hot bath, although often he had to wait for Saturday, which was bathday. Bath houses were built separately from the main farm and were a bit like steam baths or saunas. Water was thrown on to a pile of red-hot stones to make the steam. For those who liked to get really hot there was a shelf which ran round the walls high up. A Viking could lie there and swelter until he was red as a beetroot. When the bathers were all pink and rosy they might finish off by whipping themselves with bundles of twigs or even rolling in the snow.

TIME FOR BED

At the end of the evening the tables were cleared away and bedding was unrolled on the earth platforms. Important people might even have lockable wood-panelled bed cupboards.

NIGHT NIGHT

WILD WOMEN
– SO WATCH OUT!

There was no place for idle hands on a Viking farm. While Viking men were out fighting or farming, Viking women were busy from morning to night:

THINGS TO DO BY BUSY BRUNHILDE

- HELP WITH THE HAY-MAKING AND HARVEST
- DO THE COOKING, WITH THE HELP OF OTHER WOMEN AND THE SLAVES
- DO THE SPINNING AND WEAVING
- HAVE THE BABIES
- RAISE THE CHILDREN
- DO THE MILKING AND MAKE THE BUTTER AND CHEESE
- ALSO – TREAT FAMILY AND WORKERS WHEN THEY ARE SICK. MAYBE DO A BIT OF FORTUNE-TELLING. GET TIRED AND SLEEP

LOVE STUFF

A young man who was interested in a girl had to be very careful. If he showed too much interest by paying her lots of visits or writing poems to her or other such soppy behaviour, and then he didn't marry her, her father might well take *blood vengeance*. If nothing else, the young man might end up paying money. One set of laws suggested the following fines if a man touched a woman whom he wasn't meant to touch:

SHOULDER (OR JUST ABOVE THE KNEE) - 47 GRAMS OF SILVER.

ELBOW (OR LEG BETWEEN KNEE OR CALF) - 75 GRAMS OF SILVER.

WRIST OR ANKLE - 113 GRAMS OF SILVER.

THE A TO D OF GETTING MARRIED

ADORATION
It helped if a girl and a boy liked each other.

BETROTHAL
If the families of the girl and boy were agreeable there would be a betrothal meeting where the *bride-price* was fixed. This was money paid by the husband to the wife's family, which had to be repaid if there was a divorce later. If no bride-price was paid then the wife would be just a concubine. In fact one way for a man to get a concubine was simply to capture her and cart her off.

CEREMONY
The marriage ceremony included drinking of 'bridal-ale' and a feast followed by going to bed together before witnesses. Women kept their own surnames.

DIVORCE
Divorce was easily arranged and could be asked for by husband or wife. The reason for a divorce could be quite a little thing such as a wife wearing trousers or a husband wearing a girlish shirt.

STRIKTLY NO SKOOL

Viking houses must have been swarming with all the children of the wives and concubines - although not quite as swarming as they could have been; sickly babies were often left outside to die. It was not a crime to kill a baby before it had started to suck milk at the breast.

There was no such thing as a Viking school, and there was no place for a 'charcoal-chewer' - a child who lingered by the warmth of the hearth instead of working. Children were brought up tough, especially boys who were expected to like fighting. In fact it was almost a compliment to say that a little boy was quarrelsome or vengeful. Under twelve years of age, a specially quarrelsome boy could kill someone and not be punished, although his family had to pay compensation.

I ONLY KILLED HIM!

WELL THAT'S OKAY THEN.

Babies were 'baptised' by sprinkling water on them - this may have been a pagan custom before it was a Christian custom.

A Fistful of Fearsome Women

Some Viking women were peace-makers, but more often they are described in the sagas as fierce and proud. "Cold are women's counsels" said the Viking proverb.

Fredydis

Fredydis was the sister of the famous Viking, Leif Eriksson, who first explored the north-east coast of America. She travelled there with him on his second voyage. During their first winter in America she quarrelled with two brothers, Helgi and Finnbogi and then told her husband, a Greenlander called Thorvard, that the brothers had mistreated her. Fredydis persuaded her husband to attack the brothers. They were dragged from their house and murdered, together with their male followers, but this wasn't enough for Freydidis; she wanted the five women followers of the brothers killed as well. And since no one would kill them, Freydis took an axe and killed them herself.

The Red Girl

In the tenth century a fierce Viking woman, known as the Red Girl, was leader of a group of Vikings in Ireland.

Volva

Volva wasn't the name of an individual. A Volva was a female prophetess. Volvas would travel from farm to farm, sometimes in groups, and answer questions about the future. They were treated with great respect.

Aud the Deep-Minded

Aud is not known to have killed anyone, but she was a very powerful woman. After the death of her husband, a Viking king in Ireland, she led her large family to the Orkney and Faroe Islands and then to Iceland where she gained control of vast lands.

Guthrith

Guthrith was the wife of Thorfinn Karlsefni, leader of the expedition to America which included Fredydis. While in America she gave birth to the first European ever to be born there, who was named Snorri Thorfinnsson. She was a very clever woman who outlived her husband by several years after their return from America, and made a Christian pilgrimage to Rome. Having travelled between Rome, Greenland, Iceland, Norway and America she must have been one of the most widely-travelled people in the world up to that time.

What do You Like to Eat?

Check it out - are you bad Viking material? (part 2)

1 For Breakfast?
a   A bowl of cereal
b   Wild seagulls' eggs
c   A sliver of toast with marmalade

2 For Lunch?
a   Beer
b   Lots of beer
c   A low-calory salad sandwich

3 For Supper?
a   boiled cabbage
b   chocolate
c   blood soup

Answers on page 122.

HAIRY KINGS, 👑 BALD SLAVES AND ER... THING

WHO'S ON TOP - AND WHO ISN'T

POWER PEAR
Viking society was pear-shaped.

KINGS
NOBLES
FREEMEN
SLAVES

SCRUFFY SLAVES
At the bottom were the slaves. They had their hair shaved or close-cropped and wore simple white woollen clothes, but they were allowed to own property and might be given their freedom. Slaves had to watch out for the farmer's wife as well as the farmer: she ruled the roost within the walls of the farmhouse.

Slaves were thought to be stupid, dirty and cowardly. It was specially shameful to be killed by a slave. One poet gives them horrid names:

FREE MEN
Mostly farmers but could be craftsmen or traders.

AND LORDLY LORDS
At the top were the kings and powerful lords. The centre of a king's or great lord's power was his hall, which could be massive. Olaf the Peacock, descendant of Aud the Deep-Minded, had a richly-carved hall which could seat a thousand. Grouped around the lord was his family and a group of trusted warriors, called his *hird*, who received rich gifts and the booty of Viking raids, and might be given land to farm. They

feasted with him during the long winter months and fought with him in all his battles.

Members of the hird who misbehaved had to sit in the lowliest positions in the hall. Everyone was allowed to throw animal bones at them for fun.

FEUD FRENZY

Whether grouped round a powerful lord or living on their own farm, Viking warriors had four big ideas:

VENGEANCE   LOYALTY AND KINSHIP
FATE   HONOUR

What these four ideas added up to was *Feud Frenzy*. If anyone hurt your friend or your family you had to take revenge to save your honour, and that could start a quarrel or *blood-feud* between families which might go on for years. These feuds between families were common. There were enemies everywhere. Here's two Viking sayings for when you are going to a feast or you are out farming:

> *Before proceeding up the hall, study all the doorways. You never know when an enemy will be present.*
>
> *In the field no man should stir one step from where his weapons are.*

Friends and family were vital to help fight against so many enemies. To increase the size of their family, men sometimes swore blood-brotherhood, mixing their blood and earth together. From then on your blood-brother's enemy was your enemy, and your enemy was his enemy.

Feuds could end dramatically, for instance by a 'burning-in' when one party caught the other at home and burned the house down, so that people had to come out and be slaughtered or die in the flames. Or feuds might end if both parties were exhausted and agreed to accept blood-money instead of vengeance.

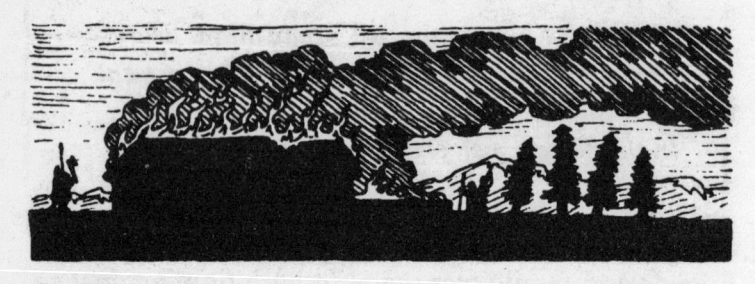

A neater way to sort out a quarrel was to agree to a duel:

1. Peg out a piece of cloth, around two metres square.

2. Dig three trenches round the cloth.

3. Place four hazel posts at the corners.

4. Take turns to strike each other.

5. Each fighter can have one friend who can protect his fighter with a shield (up to three shields can be used).

6. If blood is shed on the cloth, the wounded man can buy mercy.

7. Two feet beyond the hazel posts and you're said to be running away.

At Last er ... Thing

Quarrels were best settled at a court or *Thing*. These were assemblies of freemen which could be local or even national, like the Althing of Iceland. *Things* were a mixture of law court and parliament and mostly they were controlled by the local chiefs. When a decision was reached on a particular case, everyone clashed their weapons together to show their agreement.

Before you could take your case to a *Thing* you had to get there, and your enemies might try to ambush you on the way. It was important to gather as much support from friends and neighbours as possible before setting out. And when you got there it was best to remember that the law was more about keeping the peace than about justice. This is a Norwegian law:

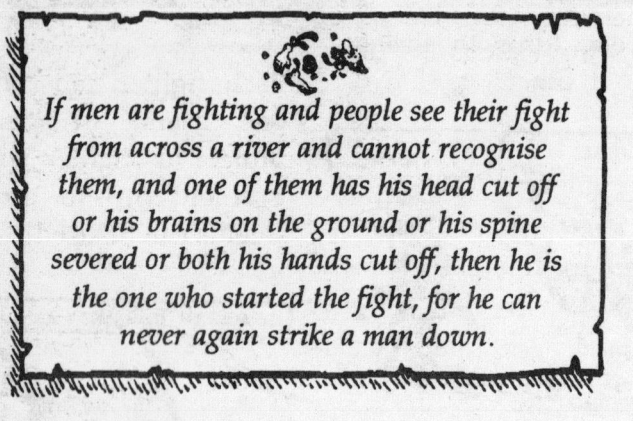

> *If men are fighting and people see their fight from across a river and cannot recognise them, and one of them has his head cut off or his brains on the ground or his spine severed or both his hands cut off, then he is the one who started the fight, for he can never again strike a man down.*

PAINFUL PUNISHMENTS

If the *Thing* found you guilty there were three kinds of punishment:

1. ATONEMENT
Every free person was classed by the amount of money they could expect to get for an injury done to them and by the amount they would have to pay if they injured someone else. Kings paid most, poor peasants paid the least.

The worse the injury, the greater the payment. The payment for a killing was called *mansbot*, but the victim's family could refuse to receive the payment and seek vengeance instead - which they tended to do, being Vikings.

GO ON TAKE IT!

2. PHYSICAL PUNISHMENT
Whipping and *mutilation* were strictly for slaves.

Hanging was for theft.

Beheading was a decent way to die for a free man.

Stoning, drowning or *sinking in a bog* were for witchcraft.

Stoning

Drowning

Sinking

3. Outlawry

As punishment for killing, a man might be declared an outlaw. This meant that he was literally outside the law. Anyone could kill him without fear of punishment, and his property went to the man who accused him. Actually it wasn't always that bad. The outlaw's friends and neighbours could protect him or he might be smuggled into exile abroad. Sometimes he was even allowed to live in a safe area near his home.

But there was never much doubt who the killer was, because if a killer had any sense he told everyone as soon as possible; a secret killing was the shameful crime of murder, while an open killing was only *manslaying*, which was nothing to be ashamed about.

ARE YOU GUILTY - OR NOT GUILTY?

Check it out - are you bad Viking material? (part 3)

Imagine you are a Viking woman and you have been accused of adultery 🐾. You have sworn that you are innocent, but the *Thing* insists that you undergo *trial by ordeal* to prove your innocence. The Vikings probably learned trial by ordeal from Christians. The idea was that God would show whether the accused was innocent or guilty. After the ordeal your wound will be bandaged for several days and then you will be judged on how clean the wound is.

WHICH DO YOU CHOOSE?

a Pick up a bar of hot iron and walk nine paces before throwing it down.
b Pick stones from a pot of boiling water.
c Cross your heart and hope to die.

Answers on page 122.

🐾 Adultery is when a married person sleeps with someone other than their husband or wife.

DRUNK AS A SCANDINAVIAN SKUNK

TIME FOR BEER AND BALLADS

Feasting was a favourite Viking hobby. They did a lot of it. The best time to feast was the start of winter when there was plenty of food left from after the harvest and not much else to do. A good feast could go on for several days.

The host made sure his guests were met with water and a towel so that they could freshen up before the feast got under way. Food was served by the women. Sometimes the lord's wife and daughters would serve with their own hands, but when things got rowdy they might clear off - if there was another room to go to.

There was plenty of food of course, but there's no doubt that the most important thing at any feast was the drink. It was ladled into drinking horns from large buckets or bowls, and the thing about a drinking horn was that if you put it down it fell over, so it had to be emptied first. The result was that all the merry-makers got blind drunk, and because the drink was full of impurities they must have had the most horrific hangovers afterwards.

The next best thing to a feast or a fight was a good story told in a poem or a saga, and the good thing about stories was that Vikings could listen to them while they were feasting, thus enjoying two of their favourite hobbies at once. Poets were stars. The biggest star of all was Egil Skallagrimsson.

LAGER SAGAS

There were two main types of poetry:
eddaic: fairly simple, all about legends and battles.
skaldic: more complicated, all about kings and battles.
Their poetry was littered with *kennings*. These were colourful names for things. For instance, the kenning for a ship might be *sea horse* or *wave-battler*. Kennings can make Viking poetry seem pretty weird. Try this short poem by the famous poet, Snorri Sturluson (answer upside down):

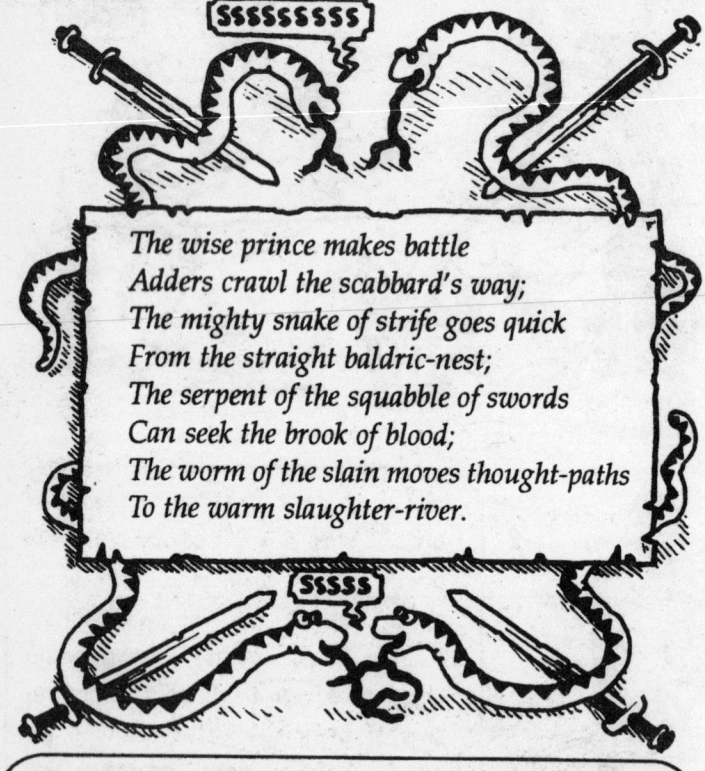

> *The wise prince makes battle*
> *Adders crawl the scabbard's way;*
> *The mighty snake of strife goes quick*
> *From the straight baldric-nest;*
> *The serpent of the squabble of swords*
> *Can seek the brook of blood;*
> *The worm of the slain moves thought-paths*
> *To the warm slaughter-river.*

Answer to poem - adders are swords, the snake of strife is a sword, the baldric-nest is its scabbard, the serpent of the squabble of swords is also a sword, as is worm of the slain. Thought-paths is the chest of an enemy, and the warm slaughter-river is lots of lovely blood for the sword to drink.

Things To Do When You're Not Drunk

When not feasting the lord and his men might play games:

Board games

A ball game played with a bat and hard ball. It could end in bloodshed.

Horse-fighting

Wrestling in water - drag your opponent under water and hold him there till he collapses.

LOONY RUNES

The Vikings had their own letters, called runes. Runes weren't much use for writing down long poems and sagas, but they were good for magic spells, and for memorials to the dead on stone and wood. They called the runic alphabet ᚠ - the *futhark* after its first six letters.

This is the key to most popular version of the *futhark*. Using it, see if you can decode the loony rune below. There are clues in the picture to help you.

Loony Rune

Answer: I am a fat bat

> Our word 'alphabet' comes from *alpha* and *beta*, the first two letters of the Greek alphabet.

WAR FEVER!

SUMMER HOLIDAYS VIKING-STYLE

The early Viking raids starting in 793 were small-scale affairs, like the first drops of rain before a storm. Local chieftains, mostly from Norway, would gather together a few warships and a small group of followers, perhaps less than a hundred. They would load up their ships with weapons, armour and food for the voyage, and set off in the spring or summer while the sea was fairly calm. It was best to get home before the winter weather set in, so they had to allow time for the return journey.

> We launched the first raids from Norway, then from around AD 830 the Danes joined in, and the fun really started. The islands of Britain and Ireland took the brunt of our attacks. Vikings started staying on over winter and looking for land to settle down on. Read these scraps from my bloodstained scrap-book.

RAIDER'S DIGEST
The voice of Vikings everywhere
Circulation 2,000,000

SHERIFF SLASHED IN PORTLAND PUNCH UP 789

The crews of three Norwegian ships have killed the Sheriff of Dorset and all his men in the small town of Portland. The Sheriff ordered our boys to come with him to the royal palace - he should have known better!

LINDISFARNE LOOTERS LEAVE TRAIL OF BLOOD 793

Norwegian raiders have plundered the lonely abbey of Lindisfarne, off the Northumberland coast, in the first proper Viking raid on English soil. The success of the raid was due to smart planning and efficient execution of the plan, leading to loads of loot and slaves. Well done boys!

MONKS MISERABLE OVER PAGAN PRIESTESS 839

A Viking chieftain, Thorgisl, has set up his headquarters at Armagh in Northern Ireland. His excellent wife has started to make pagan prophecies from the altar of the local monastery. The monks have either left or been slaughtered.

EDITORIAL

That's enough complaints from the Irish about raids on their monasteries. It's well known that they are not above a spot of raiding themselves, especially when food is short. Irish monks can be as bloodthirsty as the common people. We remind our readers of the battle in 807 between the monasteries of Cork and Clonfert, which left mounds of dead monks and superiors.

DUBLIN NAMED 836

Congratulations to the first Viking settlers in Ireland who have founded their colony at a murky spot on the River Liffey. It's been named Dubb-Lin meaning Black Pool. The new town is expected to become a major base for the slave trade and for raiding into England.

DORESTADT DESTROYED BY DANISH DEVILS 834

The Vikings have opened their onslaught on the Frankish empire of mainland Europe with a devilishly devastating attack on the town of Dorestadt.

PARIS PLUNDERERS PAID PROTECTION MONEY 845

We understand that Charles the Bald, Emperor of the Franks, has paid 3,000 Kg of silver to a Viking army for them to leave Paris, in the first known payment of Danegeld in France.

DAMN IT THANET! 850

For the first time Danish Vikings have stayed over winter on the Isle of Thanet on the coast of Kent. This could be the start of a new trend for Vikings in England. We'll keep you posted.

GETTING TOOLED UP

There were laws saying what weapons a Viking had to take with him on a raid. In Sweden it was a shield, sword, spear and iron hat, and a mail coat or leather jerkin, a bow and a dozen arrows for each rowing bench of the ship.

THE COMPLETE VIKING

- HELMET
- 'TWISTING SPEAR', PERHAPS THROWN WITH A CORD SO THAT IT ROTATED IN FLIGHT.
- CHAIN-MAIL SHIRT OR PADDED LEATHER JERKIN WHICH MIGHT HAVE PIECES OF BONE SEWN INTO IT.
- METAL SHIELD RIM — BUT NOT TOO HEAVY, THE SHIELD HAD TO BE QUITE LIGHT
- IRON SHIELD BOSS FOR EXTRA KNUCKLE PROTECTION
- ROUND SHIELD MADE OF THIN WOODEN BOARDS HELD TOGETHER BY AN IRON BAR ONE METRE ACROSS. LEATHER COVER PAINTED IN BRIGHT COLOURS
- SWORD IN WOODEN SCABBARD LINED WITH OILED LEATHER OR WAXED CLOTH.
- 'BEARDED' AXE — WITH HOOK FOR GRAPPLING.

Swords were the favourite Viking weapon. They were given special names such as *Snake of Wounds* or *Leg-Biter* and were handed down from father to son. The best swords were made by pattern-welding. This made the steel extra hard by increasing the amount of carbon in the metal.

How to Pattern-Weld a Sword

1. Thin bars of iron were kept red-hot in charcoal to absorb carbon, which charcoal is formed from. Steel is a mixture of iron and carbon and is stronger than iron.

2. The bars were repeatedly cut up, twisted together and reheated.

3. The red-hot, twisted bars were hammered together to make the central part of a swordblade.

4. Two red-hot strips of finest steel were hammered on to make the cutting edges.

5. The blade was 'quenched' to make it harder still. This meant plunging it into a cold liquid, perhaps honey or oil.

6. The edges were filed sharp and the blade polished by rubbing with vinegar or urine.

Swords weighed between one and two kilos and a skilful swordsman could fight with either hand, switching from left to right to confuse his enemy. For a Viking, skill with a sword counted for more than skill with a ball for a professional footballer today - it had to: his life depended on it.

SWORD TIPS FOR STARTERS

🗡 The important thing is to be strong and fast on your feet like a boxer, keep ducking and weaving, and take big leaps sideways and backwards to avoid having your legs slashed off.

🗡 Aim heavy slashing blows at your opponent's head or limbs. Try to hack off an arm or a leg.

🗡 Hold your shield well out from the body.
It's best to ward off blows with the flat of the shield and not with the iron rim. Your opponent may break his sword on the rim if you're lucky, but if he cuts through the rim he's pretty certain to split your shield in two.

🗡 Fight with the sun behind you, so that your opponent is blinded by the sun in his eyes.

🗡 Don't forget - in a formal duel you're allowed two more shields if the first gets broken.

GETTING STUCK IN

Battles started with a hail of arrows, spears or stones but soon broke up into a scrum of individual duels. One tactic was to form a *swine array* which meant marching forward in a wedge formation with the best men in the 'snout'. Another was to form a defensive 'shieldwall' if the battle was going against you. Later Vikings learned to use battering rams and catapults for attacking cities.

Most kings and leaders didn't live long. They fought at the front of a battle surrounded by trusty warriors, where the fighting was thickest.

Skilled fighters were highly-respected. One amazing skill was to catch a spear in mid-air with a back-hand stroke, swing right round in a circle and fling the spear back at your enemy, all in one movement.

Another trick was to throw a spear from each hand. The famous Viking king, Olaf Trygvasson, could do this.

BEAR-NAKED

One type of fighter was especially feared. This was the *berserker*. Berserk means bear-shirt. These were fighters dedicated to the god Odin, whose name meant furious or mad. They worked themselves up into a fighting madness by rhythmic howling and jumping (and possibly with drink) then fought naked in a *berserk rage*, not caring whether they lived or died. They were unstoppable in battle, but they were looked on with horror by normal Vikings and were probably nasty bullies in normal life.

STEINTHOR'S STORY

One saga tells of how a skilled warrior called Steinthor saved his friend's life. During a battle Steinthor's friend was fighting on ice when he slipped and fell over. As an enemy warrior prepared to finish the friend off, Steinthor ran forward, held up his own shield over his friend to ward off the enemy blow, while with his other hand he slashed off the enemy's leg, and 'in one and the same moment' leapt in the air so that a blow aimed at him by another enemy warrior passed safely beneath his legs.

Vikings weren't bothered about death or dead bodies. There's an Irish description of a Viking victory feast after a battle in about 880: *the army encamped on the very battlefield to cook their food. The cauldrons were placed on top of heaps of fallen Norwegians, with spits stuck in among the bodies, and the fires burning them so that their bellies burst, revealing the welter of beef and pork eaten the night before.*

SPOT THE SPARE LIMB!

In this picture there's one limb more than there ought to be. Can you see which it is?

FEARSOME FORTS

There could be more to Viking military technique than a berserk charge by wild men in 'swine array'. Some Viking kings had standing armies. In Denmark there were four great military camps, all built to the same design. Each could house some five and a half thousand warriors. They were built late in the Viking Age after the days of small scale raiders were over.

As well as camps for their warriors, the Danish kings built defensive fortifications. The biggest was the Danevirke, a huge rampart which stretched for nearly fourteen kilometres across the bottom of Denmark.

> The Danevirke had one opening - enough to let a road pass through it - in case the Danes wished to march south. After all, the Danes could raid south overland if they wanted to; all the other Vikings had no choice but to go by water ...

ROW, ROW, ROW, THE BOAT

A Fight on the Ocean Wave

Nowhere in Denmark is further than fifty-six kilometres from the ocean and Norway is narrow too. So the sea was on the Vikings' doorstep and they needed it like a joy-rider needs the open road. They learned to build ships as beautiful as swans, but a lot more dangerous.

On an average raid there might be up to sixty warships, or *longships* as they are known. The longships were fast and sleek. Under sail they could reach speeds of more than sixteen kilometres per hour, which is not bad for a wind-powered ship. They carried forty oarsmen or more. The *Long Serpent* of

King Olaf Trygvason, built in the winter of AD 999, had sixty-four oarsmen. These sailors were always free men, unlike the crews of slave-galleys in the Mediterranean Sea. The captain had to be careful how he treated them.

The very first boats in Scandinavia were made of leather stretched over a wooden frame, but these were to the Viking longship what a pedal-bike is to a high-powered motorbike. By 350 BC early versions of the longship, like the Hjortspring ship, were being built with most of the features of Viking-age ships.

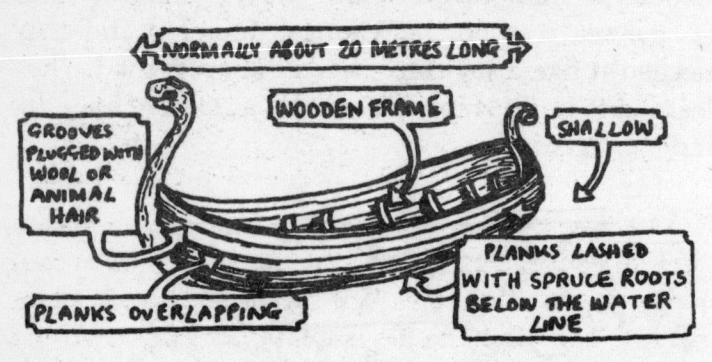

Diagram of a longship with labels:
- NORMALLY ABOUT 20 METRES LONG
- WOODEN FRAME
- SHALLOW
- GROOVES PLUGGED WITH WOOL OR ANIMAL HAIR
- PLANKS OVERLAPPING
- PLANKS LASHED WITH SPRUCE ROOTS BELOW THE WATER LINE

The Hjortspring ship was *clinker-built* of overlapping planks. It had twenty oars but no sail; sails were added by the Vikings. The longships were shallow-bottomed, which meant that they could be drawn up silently on any shelving beach and they could be sailed up shallow rivers to strike deep inland.

As well as using their ships for inland raids, it seems that the Vikings also used them for sea battles. In a sea battle the ships of a fleet might be lashed together to give a firm footing for the warriors, and some ships might have an iron frame lashed to the front end to act as a ram. Wooden screens were tied to the sides to fend off arrows.

Sea battles began with a storm of arrows and spears, then the ships crashed together and warriors sprang forward across the bows. The men in the bows did the hand-to-hand fighting; it was a mark of honour to be a 'stem-dweller', and row in the bows of the ship. Those at the back fired arrows over the heads of the fighters and waited to take the places of those who fell.

KNORR v. LONGSHIP BEAUTY CONTEST

Which do you prefer?

We know a lot about Viking ships, especially from the remains of three longships taken from Norwegian burial mounds: the Osberg, Gokstad and Tune ships. As well as longships, the Vikings

LONGSHIP

DETACHABLE FIGUREHEAD. IT WAS THOUGHT TO BE BAD LUCK TO LAND WITH IT ATTACHED.

SMALL DINGHY

20 METRES LONG

LEATHER BUCKET FOR BAILING

SEA-SICK VIKING

also built *knorrs*, or cargo-ships. Knorrs were shorter and stubbier than longships, with wide middle sections to hold cargo. They were very sea-worthy and useful. Vikings loved them. The greatest compliment that a Viking could pay to a beautiful woman was to call her 'knorr-breasted'.

KNORR

GILDED WEATHER VANE

SIDE TILLER

15 METRES LONG

CARGO HOLD

ROUNDED OR 'SWAN-BREASTED' AT THE FRONT.

A Night on the Ocean Wave

For all their skill as sailors the sea was still a very dangerous place for Vikings. We know of at least one knorr which was tossed right up in the air by the waves and landed bottom up.

On a dark night on the Atlantic Ocean, when the waves were high as a house, a longship wasn't a very comfortable place to be either. The warriors sat hunched on their sea-chests, their cloaks wrapped around them. They might hoist a long tent on the deck and snuggle down in two-man leather sleeping bags to snatch what sleep they could out of the spray and wind. But it was impossible to cook on board ship if they wanted a hot meal, so if they could, they preferred to pull in to the nearest shore at night and to pitch their tents on dry land.

So Long, Longships

For three hundred years longships ruled the sea-lanes of northern Europe. But eventually new ship-designs caught up with them. Other countries started to build ships higher out of the water. This meant that in a sea battle they could fight the Vikings from above, which was a big advantage in the days of spears and bows and arrows. The Vikings tried building fighting-platforms at the front and back of their ships, but their enemies just built platforms on their higher ships and kept the advantage of height. Finally, after several hundred years, the Viking longship ceased to rule the seas of Northern Europe.

GO WEST, YOUNG MAN

BUT FIRST, YOU HAVE TO KNOW THE WAY...

If you're rocking in a small boat in the middle of a vast ocean it's very hard to know where you are or which way to go. Despite this, and without any modern aids to navigation, the Vikings travelled all over the North Atlantic without great difficulty. Some of their directions for even the longest journeys seem amazingly casual:

> HOW DO I GET TO GREENLAND FROM NORWAY?

> EASY. I COULD DO IT WITH MY EYES CLOSED: JUST HEAD WEST AND DON'T STOP TILL YOU GET THERE. TRY NOT TO BUMP INTO ICELAND.

THINGS VIKINGS DIDN'T HAVE

- Ship's compasses
- Radar
- Satellite positioning systems
- Sonar

THINGS VIKINGS DID HAVE

◊ A knowledge of the sea

◊ A bearing dial, for working out direction relevant to the sun or the North Star.

◊ On overcast days they may have looked for the sun with a type of see-through stone which became cloudy when pointed towards the light.

◊ Luck

Sometimes they got it wrong. In fact most of the great Viking discoveries were made by seamen who had been blown off course ...

THE FAROES AND BEYOND

Having attacked Ireland, mainland Britain and the Orkney Islands, the Vikings were ready for longer voyages far out of sight of land.

The Faroes are a bleak chain of islands which jut from the ocean like rotten teeth halfway between Scotland and Iceland. Some time around 820 a Viking called Grim Kamban visited them. He probably sailed there from Ireland, as his second name is an Irish nickname meaning *crooked*. The only people he found living on the Faroes were some Irish monks, known to the Vikings as *Papar* ◤.

The Papars liked the Faroe Islands, describing with pleasure how in summer when the sun hardly set they could pick the lice from their shirts in the middle of the night. Papars were brave but they were dead unfriendly. Their custom had been to launch out to sea in tiny round leather-covered boats called *currachs* and let the wind and the waves take them. With luck they would bump into an empty island where they would build a tiny shed and live with just a few sheep for company - and strictly no other people nearby.

More Scandinavians soon followed Grim Kamban to the Faroes, and the Papars left. Nowadays the capital of the Faroes is called *Torshavn* - or *Thor's Haven*, after the Norse god *Thor*.

'Not a Nice Land - Iceland' (says Floki)

After the Faroes, the next step for the Vikings was Iceland, halfway to America - well almost. The first Viking to spot it was probably a Swede called Gadar who was blown there while sailing from the Hebrides to the Faroes in 880. Or it may have been a Viking

---

◤ Papar meant father.

called Nadod who was blown off-course while sailing from Norway to the Faroes in 860. Either way, other Vikings soon followed.

THE TALE OF FLOKI AND THE RELUCTANT RAVENS

Iceland was called Iceland by the explorer, Floki, who was the first to try and settle there, but took a dislike to it. Floki took three sacred ravens with him when he set sail from the Faroes. He released the first raven once he was well out to sea but it flew straight back to land. Then having sailed a little further, he released the second - but it flew back to the ship. Finally he released the third raven and it flew straight ahead. He followed it - to Iceland.

Unfortunately Floki forgot to bring any hay with him so that his cows, sheep and horses died over winter. He and his crew had a terrible winter and left as soon as possible in the spring. He called the land Iceland in disgust, but it was his own fault that he couldn't stay there. He should have brought the right provisions with him.

Iceland was an empty country when Floki arrived, except for a few Papars who soon left. A flood of settlers followed him, bringing their families, slaves and followers with them. Four hundred leading men and three thousand of their families and followers are recorded in a book called the Landnamabok, in a detailed record of the first settlers.

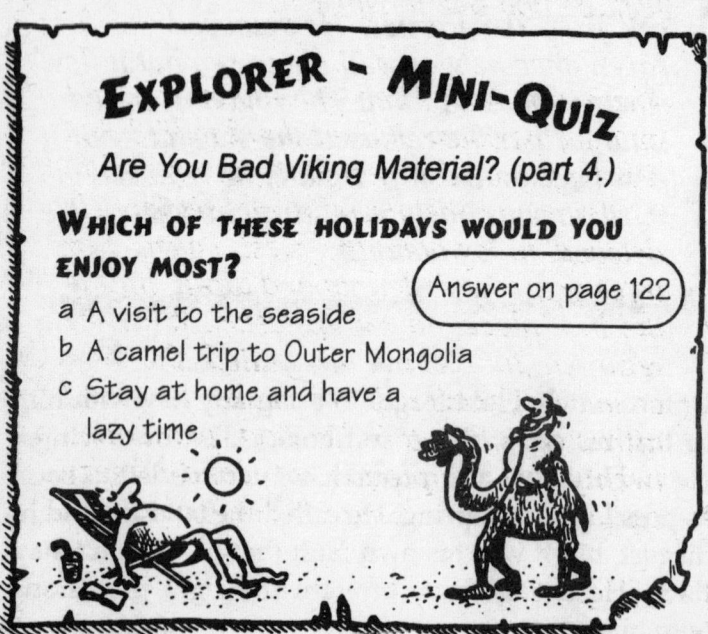

NO PEACE AND QUIET NOWADAYS

I HATE PEOPLE - AND THAT INCLUDES YOU!

EXPLORER - MINI-QUIZ

Are You Bad Viking Material? (part 4.)

WHICH OF THESE HOLIDAYS WOULD YOU ENJOY MOST?

a A visit to the seaside
b A camel trip to Outer Mongolia
c Stay at home and have a lazy time

Answer on page 122

THE TALE OF ERIK AND THE NOT-SO GREENLAND

In 982 a red-haired man-killer called Erik the Red decided to check out the rumours of a new land in the west, told to him by a sailor called Gunnbjorn who had seen land while storm-driven fifty years before. Eric was eager to search for this new land because he had to leave Iceland in a hurry, having just killed someone. It was becoming a habit. The same thing had happened twice before, another killing in Iceland and one in Norway.

There may have been an attempt to settle on the east coast of Greenland in 978, but a savagely cold winter had put an end to it. Erik was the first proper settler. He decided to explore the west coast. For three years he sailed up and down, noting the best places to set up farms. When he returned to Iceland he called the new country 'Greenland' to make it sound attractive. By 986 he had persuaded twenty-five shiploads of land-hungry settlers to follow him to the new country.

The number of Norse people living on Greenland grew to over four thousand at its peak. They traded with Inuit, or Eskimos, in the far north and kept in contact with Iceland and Norway back home. Mainly they lived by farming; there were a hundred and ninety farms strung out along the west coast, rearing cattle, sheep and goats. The site of Erik's farm, *Bratahlith*, can still be seen. It is overgrown with grass and surrounded by the ruins of later farm buildings.

But a farming life wasn't enough for Erik's family. They needed something more ...

AMERICA!

Erik the Red's son, Leif Eriksson was called *Leif the Lucky*. He heard tell of a land to the west of Greenland from a Viking called Bjarni. In 986 Bjarni had set out from Iceland for Greenland and missed it in a fog, sighting a strange coast before turning back. Bjarni was probably the first European ever to see America, more than five hundred years before Columbus.

Around 1003 Leif bought Bjarni's ship ⬤ and they set sail together from the farm at Bratahlith. They saw

> He may have bought the ship in the belief that it would 'know the way', having been there before.

three new countries, which they called Slab Land, Forest Land and Wine Land (Vinland). Vinland was given its name because wild grapes grew there. It was where the Vikings landed. It may have been New England. In the words of the Greenlanders' Saga:

> *They went ashore and looked about them. The weather was fine. There was dew on the grass, and the first thing they did was to get some of it on their hands and put it to their lips, and to them it seemed the sweetest thing they had ever tasted.*

They found wild wheat, timber and grapes and lots of salmon and decided to stay the winter, sailing home to Greenland in the spring with a cargo of timber and dried grapes.

WE'VE COME TO STAY

Back home in Greenland, Leif got busy organising a bigger expedition, and after a few years he set out with a hundred and sixty people in three ships. Bjarni, the first European to sight America, was one of the party.

Things got off to a poor start when one of the leaders, Thorhall the Hunter (who was a bit mad) became really unpleasant and said that they were looking for Vinland in the wrong direction. He sailed off in one of the ships and eventually reached Ireland where he and his men were tortured and used as slaves by the Irish.

The Vikings who made it to Vinland stayed there only three years. They were plagued by quarrels over women and attacks by native Americans or Indians - *Skraeling* or *screechers* as the Vikings called them - who killed Leif's brother, Thorvald.

Bad trouble started after the second winter when a Skraeling was killed by a Viking while trying to steal some Viking weapons. The Skraelings sought revenge and attacked the Vikings with a large catapult handled by several men. It threw a dark-coloured ball ⬛ and killed one man. The Vikings retreated, but were rallied by Erik the Red's daughter, Freydidis who grabbed the

dead man's sword. Two Vikings and four Skraelings were killed in the battle that followed. From then on the Vikings were always in danger from native Americans.

They decided to make a new camp on an island further north where they would be safer from the Skraelings. But they quarrelled endlessly over women and in the summer they decided to give up and go home. Bjarni, who had started it all, was drowned in the Irish sea trying to get back to Greenland.

> The Algonquin tribe of native Americans have a tradition that their ancestors had such a weapon. It threw a boulder sewn into a skin.

FORGOTTEN HEROES

For hundreds of years no one knew for sure that the Vikings had discovered America. It was just a story written in two ancient Icelandic sagas, the Greenlanders' Saga and Erik's Saga. Now there's no doubt:

> Clue no 1:
> Remains of Viking longhouses found at L'Anse-aux-Meadows on Newfoundland.

> Clue no 2:
> Indian arrowhead found in Greenland.

> Clue no 3:
> A Viking coin found in New England.

ALL RIGHT THEN, GO EAST!

RAIDERS IN RIVER BOATS

While Norwegians raided and traded in the west, Swedes did the same in the east, and the Danes did a bit of both. There was a bit less raiding and a bit more trading in the east on the whole, but like all healthy Vikings, the Swedes and Danes could turn their hand to either as it suited them.

The eastern Vikings traded over huge distances. The small figure of a Buddha from far-away India has been

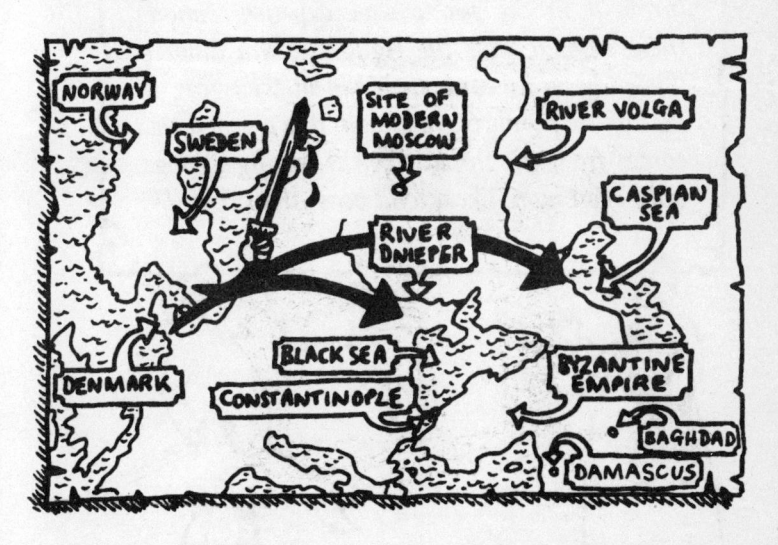

found in Sweden along with great glittering hoards of eastern coins and other goods. They traded with Arab countries and with the mighty Byzantine Empire. Wealth from the eastern trade flooded back into Denmark and Sweden in a great shiny river of gold and silver. Three large Viking towns called Ribe, Birka and Hedeby grew out of this trading wealth.

Hedeby was the largest town. It was at the Scandinavian end of several long trade routes to Arab lands far in the south, where slaves, amber, walrus ivory and furs were sold, and wine and other southern luxuries were bought. A visiting Arab called Ibrahim ibn Ahmed a'Tartushi left a description of Hedeby in the 950s. He thought the Vikings were savages:

> *A very large town beyond the furthest end of the ocean. When a child is born they often throw it in the sea to save expense. Among them women have the right to claim divorce. Never have I heard such hideous singing as that of the people of this town; it is a growl that comes from the throat like the baying of dogs, only even more like a wild beast than that.*

But the people of Hedeby were more than savages. Most lived in small square houses which stood in rows on either side of wooden roads, each with its own well and fenced-in courtyard. Many were craftsmen making jewels, decorated weapons and ornaments from materials such as soapstone, glass, amber, silver and walrus ivory.

Vikings liked to smother the things they made in swirling, crawling patterns. There were many different styles. Here are some of them:

Ringerike

Urnes

Mammen

Jellinge

A-Mazing Gripping Beasts

The Viking Age started with the Gripping Beast style where strange animals or people clutch at each other and themselves with hands, feet and paws. Other styles used weaving winding lines like drawn-out knitting. This picture is made up from a bit of both. *Follow the line which ends at the bottom of page 83.*

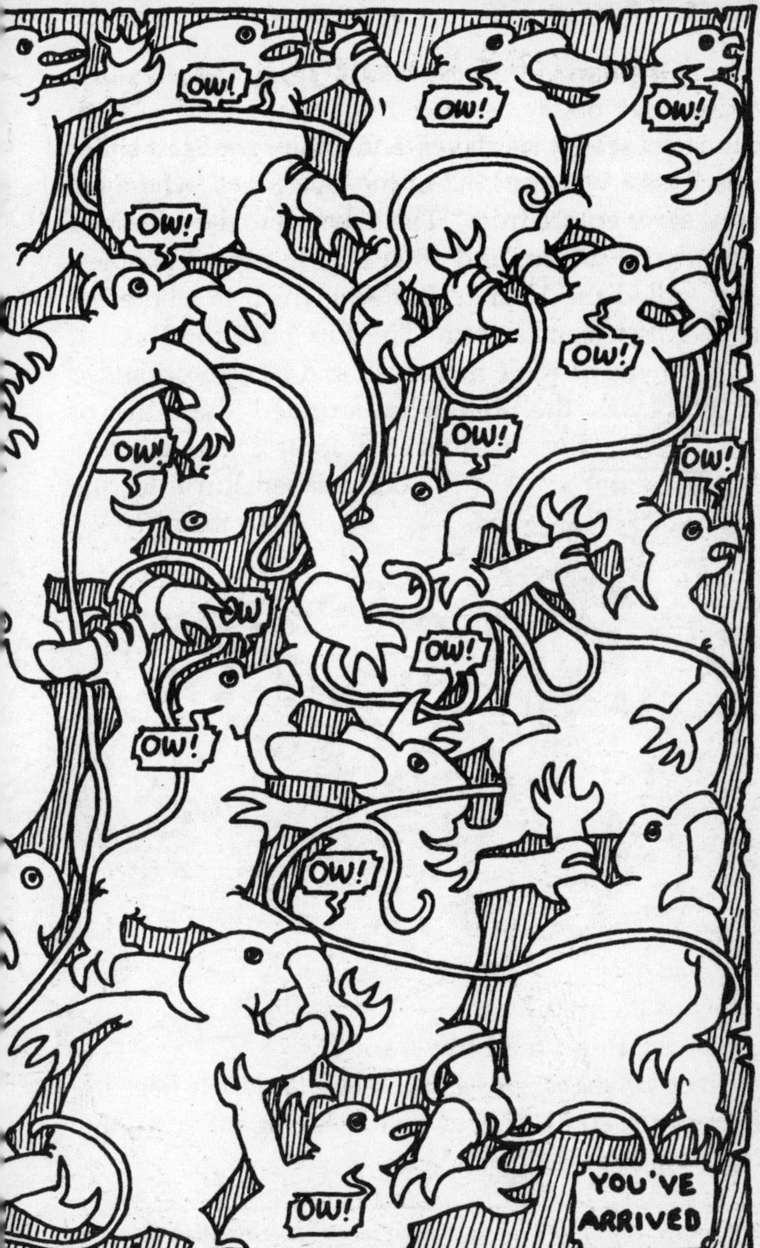
OW!
OW!
OW!
OW!
OW!
OW!
OW!
OW!
OW
OW!
OW!
OW!
OW!
YOU'VE ARRIVED

NEVER TRUST A RUS

From Denmark, and especially from Sweden, the Vikings set off across the huge wastes of western Russia in search of slaves and other goods. At that time Russia was the land of the wild Slavs (where the word slave comes from). The Slavs were the ancestors of modern Russians and other East-European peoples. They called the Vikings *Rus* ◂, which is where the name *Russia* comes from. The Rus built the Russian towns of Kiev, Smolensk and Novgorod and it was the Rus who founded the state of Russia, after the local Slavs asked a Viking called Rurik to rule for them.

When they had gathered their trade-goods, the Rus would travel south, by river whenever possible, assembling their fleet at a fortress just south of Kiev before setting off down the River Volga to the Black Sea.

Rus was possibly a Finnish word for a Swede before the Slavs got hold of it.

> **RUS TOILET FACT**
> The Arab, Ibn Rustah, said that the Rus lived in such a state of distrust among themselves that a man could not leave his house to go to the toilet without an armed escort.

Once on the river they drifted downstream using local boats. When they came to rapids they would let most of the people walk, leaving their goods in the boats, while the boatmen plunged into the water naked, steering the boats with poles. If the water was specially difficult they would carry both goods and boats overland until the water was calmer again.

Some Arabs travelled north in order to meet them half way and these Arabs left the earliest descriptions of the eastern Vikings. The Rus wore wide baggy eastern trousers and were very handsome and clean according to one Arab (although another describes them as repulsively dirty in their personal habits, so we're not completely sure). They kept lots of slave girls, sacrificed men, women and cattle to their gods, usually by hanging, and were quarrelsome. Sword or axe duels were common.

The eastern Vikings spread their net wide. They travelled far south and east into Muslim territory, destroying the Khazar town of Abasgun on the southern shore of the Caspian Sea around 864. But their favourite destination was Constantinople (now Istanbul), the capital of the Byzantine Empire ...

THE GREAT CITY

Constantinople, or *Mikligardr* (the Great City), as the Vikings called it, was on the southern tip of the Black Sea, and was the largest city in the world. It had half a million inhabitants. It was shiny with gold and had so many churches they were like molehills in a meadow. Constantinople drew the Rus like wasps to a jam-pot.

The Rus reached Constantinople by 838. By the 860s a Rus fleet had ravaged the towns along the shores of the Black Sea and appeared before the walls of the Great City, only to be defeated by a violent storm. In 907 they were back again - and again. But the Rus never captured Constantinople: the Byzantines were too crafty. They made a treaty with the Rus in 911-12 which covered things like murder, theft and shipwreck (there was already some sort of arrangement for free baths). The Rus were allowed to spend the summer in the suburbs of the city but they could not enter the city proper in groups of more than fifty men, and they had to be unarmed. After the treaty of 911-12 the Byzantines were able to deal fairly peacefully with the Rus - well, most of the time anyway.

THE TALE OF IGOR AND THE FLAME THROWERS

In 941, after thirty years of peace, a Rus chieftain called Igor attacked Constantinople with a large fleet. The Byzantines only had fifteen broken-down galleys to fight him with, but they were crafty as ever. They loaded their galleys with a chemical mixture called Greek Fire packed into wooden tubes cased in bronze. Then, the current being in the right direction, they let the galleys drift down on the Rus fleet. As the galleys closed the Byzantine crews squirted water at the bases of the wooden tubes. This had the effect of 'firing' them. Flames arched over the Rus ships. Thousands leapt into the water and those who reached the shore were slaughtered. The Rus kept the peace for some time after this defeat.

Rus were useful in the Byzantine Emperor's bodyguard, which was soon packed with large fair-haired men and became known as the *Varangian Guard*. Varangian was what the Byzantines called the Vikings. As Varangians the Vikings fought for Byzantium in the area of modern Iraq and even attacked Athens. If you want proof, there's a stone lion in Venice which was taken from Athens and has Viking graffiti on it.

> There's another way of getting to the east from Scandinavia. Sail south down the coast of Europe, turn left at the Straits of Gibraltar and keep straight on down the Mediterranean Sea. Take a look at these cuttings from my scrap-book!

RAIDER'S DIGEST
The voice of Vikings everywhere
Circulation 2,000,000

SEVILLE SLAUGHTER 844
Viking raiders have attacked the Spanish city of Seville, ruled by the Moors of North Africa. The men of the city are said to have been killed, and the women and children taken captive. Regrettably, latest reports say the Vikings have been defeated by the Moors and have retreated to France.

LUNA LOSERS IN MASSACRE MIX-UP 860
Top Viking chiefs Bjorn and Hastein have sacked the city of Luna in Italy mistaking it for the city of Rome because of its gleaming white walls. They tricked their way into the city by pretending to be refugees needing to bury their chief. Once inside the city, Hastein leapt from his coffin and led a splendid killing-feast in the narrow streets.

RAIDERS RETURN 862
Top chiefs Bjorn and Hastein have returned from a long trip to the Mediterranean Sea. They may have reached Egypt during their travels. Their ships are laden with slaves and booty from raids in Spain, Italy and North Africa. It is rumoured that their African captives or 'blue men' are to be sold as slaves in Ireland.

THE BULLDOG BITES BACK

BRITAIN AT BATTLE-STATIONS - THE STORY SO FAR

1 Britain and Europe had been flattened by Viking raiders for over fifty years: raiders like Ragnar who attacked Paris in 845, withdrawing only after being offered seven thousand pounds of silver.

2 Society was breaking up under Viking attack. A monk wrote: any slave runs away from his master and, deserting Christianity, becomes a Viking.

3 Europe started to defend itself, building defensive bridges across rivers and fortifying towns.

4 In England the Saxon Kingdoms were weak and divided.

5 In 865 a 'Great Heathen Army' 🐾 looking for easier pickings landed in England from Europe. It was led by the sons of Ragnar, seeking vengeance for his execution by the Saxon king, Ella, in a snake-pit in York a few years before. As Ragnar said in the snake-pit: *the piglets would be grunting if they knew what was happening to the boar.*

THE SONS OF RAGNAR
- IVAR THE BONELESS
- HALFDAN
- UBBI

6 In 866 the Viking army captured York and took revenge for the death of Ragnar by carving the *blood-eagle* on the back of King Ella. They cut his ribs from his spine, pulled out his lungs and spread them on his back so they looked like the wings of an eagle. It may have been a sacrifice to the Viking god, Odin.

7 For the next few years the Vikings rampaged almost unchecked around England and carved out a kingdom for themselves, know as *Danelaw*, based in York.

> 🐾 Armies at this date were actually very small. The Great Heathen Army was probably around five hundred men.

ENTER THE HERO

Meanwhile in 871 Alfred, England's greatest king ever (in fact the only one to be called *Great*), became king of the Saxon kingdom of Wessex at the young age of twenty-two or twenty-three. Wessex was so weak when Alfred came to the throne that in 875, when the Vikings mounted their usual rampage, he had to hide all summer in the Somerset marshes at Athelney.

FAMOUS CAKE STORY

I CAN'T TURN MY BACK ON YOU FOR A MINUTE!

While he was hiding in the Somerset marshes, Alfred did a lot of his planning for the reconquest of England. The story goes that once he hid in the hut of a peasant woman. She asked him to watch some cakes that she was cooking while she went out, but Alfred was so deep in thought that he burned the cakes. When she came back she told him off.

ALFRED'S PROBLEM

The Vikings could raid anywhere at any time. It was impossible to know where they would strike first and to have an army ready in the right place to fight them.

Alfred's people were Saxon farmers. They could not stay in the army all year; they had to look after their farms, and when they were busy farming they were easy prey for the Vikings.

ALFRED'S SOLUTION

Alfred and his successors built a network of fortified towns and strong-points, called *burghs*, all over his kingdom. The plan was that in case of Viking attack no one would be more than a day's walk away from somewhere safe, so most Burghs were about thirty kilometres apart. These burghs were the start of many English towns. If you live in a town ending in -burgh or -bury, then now you know how it started.

! He created England's first navy, building ships to his own design. They were bigger than Viking ships, with sixty oars, and higher out of the water, which was better for sea battles.

> He split his army in half. One lot stayed at home while the other half fought. That way there was always someone to fight and someone to do the farming.

! In 886 the Saxon kingdom of Mercia accepted Alfred's leadership so that he controlled most of Saxon-held England.

! But fighting wasn't all that our hero was interested in. At that time most writing was in Latin, but Alfred wanted people to write in Anglo-Saxon as well, the language which modern English grew from. He asked his Welsh friend, Bishop Asser, to start the *Anglo-Saxon Chronicle*, which is how we know so much about the Viking raids on

England. On top of this, Alfred made all his top noblemen learn to read and write. No wonder he was called Great; he helped create a lot of our towns and our language.

WHEN IS A VIKING NOT A VIKING?

Since Alfred had made raiding difficult, the Vikings - or Danes as they were now known - decided to stay peacefully in their kingdom of Danelaw and its capital, York. The Danelaw was accepted by Alfred in a treaty with the leader of the Danes, Guthrum, in 878.

In fact by 878 most of the Danes in Danelaw weren't Viking raiders at all. They were just ordinary settlers. They even left the Saxons unharmed in their villages and cleared unused land to start their own farms. Villages and farms in what was once Danelaw still often have Danish names. Danes even copied Saxon farming methods, including the *open field system*, which is not farming based on leaving gates open, but a method of sharing huge fields.

Soon Danes and Saxons started mixing and their descendants all became English men and women. In fact modern English is based on the way people spoke in the East Midlands, where Danes and Saxons mixed most freely.

> But if you think everyone lived happily ever after, think again ...

DISASTER STRIKES AGAIN!

ENGLAND – THE STORY SO FAR

1 878-899 King Alfred triumphed over the Danes in many battles.

2 After Alfred's death his successors bravely kept up the fight.

3 In 954 the last Viking king of York, Eric Bloodaxe, was driven from his kingdom, although the Danish settlers were allowed to stay.

4 Then came more than twenty years of peace.

> Peace! – You'll be lucky. Take a look at these pages from RAIDER'S DIGEST!

RAIDER'S DIGEST

The voice of Vikings everywhere
Circulation 2,000,000

WE'RE BACK! 980

We are very pleased to announce the first successful Viking raid on England in more than twenty years. The town of Southampton has been sacked and most of its people killed or taken captive. Excellent work, Vikings!

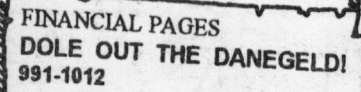

LONDON'S BURNING! 982

Following resumption of raiding in 980 we are delighted to report that the city of London has been burned down following a raid for loot and slaves.

FINANCIAL PAGES
DOLE OUT THE DANEGELD! 991-1012

Overflowing treasure chests in Scandinavia may lead to inflation if raiding continues. Danegelds paid out by English kings have been getting bigger, rising from £10,000 in 991 to £48,000 in 1012. Someone should have told them – 'once you start paying the Danegeld, you never get rid of the Dane!'

MALDON MAYHEM 991

Viking hero Olaf Trygvasson has smashed a Saxon army at Maldon in Essex. The Saxons are said to have fought bravely but they were no match for our brave boys. A Saxon poem is now being written about the battle.

MASSACRE! 1002

All Danes living in England, men, women and children, have been massacred on the orders of Saxon king, Ethelred the Unready. It is said that the sister of King Svein Forkbeard of Denmark is among the victims.

WHAT A LAF! OLAF! 1009

Viking king, Olaf Haraldsson, has torn down London Bridge by pulling at it with grappling irons attached to his ships. A song has been written about it. 'London Bridge is falling down, falling down, falling down'

ARCHBISHOP AXED 1011

Never let it be said that our brave boys are without mercy. Reports have just reached us of how newly-Christian Viking Thrum has helped the Archbishop of Canterbury to heaven. It seems that following the capture of Canterbury our boys found a store of wine and got very drunk. Understandably they became a little out of hand and started to pelt the Archbishop to death with bones and ox-heads. Thrum, seeing the archbishop's problem, put him out of his misery with an axe-blow to the head.

FORKBEARD FIGHTS BACK 1013

Danish Viking king, Svein Forkbeard, having returned to England to take revenge for Ethelred's massacre, has completed the conquest of the country in time for Christmas. At last the whole country has fallen to the Vikings. Congratulations, comrades!

THE END GAME

Svein Forkbeard had succeeded in conquering England by Christmas 1013, but he didn't live long enough to enjoy it. He died in February 1014. After a bit more fighting his son, King Canute, took the throne and ruled over both England and Denmark.

CANUTE

(LONG BENT NOSE, HANDSOME, STRONG, FAIR, TALL)

Canute turned out to be quite a good king and England had twenty more years of peace.

FAMOUS CANUTE STORY

One day King Canute's chair was taken down to the coast. He sat down in it and ordered the tide to turn back. It didn't of course. It's said that his courtiers had persuaded him to do this out of flattery, to show that he was such an incredibly powerful king that even the sea obeyed him. Actually Canute wanted to show his courtiers that only God can control the tide - Canute was a Christian.

Hard Harald Stories

Canute died in 1035 and an English king, Edward the Confessor, soon took the throne of England. But other Vikings didn't give up without a struggle. Harald Hardrada 👺 (means Hard Ruler, he was also known as Harald the Ruthless) prepared to attack in 1066. Harald was a ferocious Viking chief.

RUTHLESS HARALD AND THE BURNING BIRDS

At the age of eighteen Harald moved to Constantinople and joined the Byzantine Emperor's Varangian Guard, bringing with him a following of five hundred warriors. He fought for the Byzantines in Palestine and Sicily and was soon on the way to establishing his reputation for ruthlessness. One saga describes his cruel trick for taking a Sicilian town. He ordered bird-catchers to collect a number of small birds. Their wings were then smeared with sulphur and wax, and wood-shavings stuck to them. The shavings were then set alight and the birds released so that they flew back to their nests in the town and set light to the thatched roofs of the defenders' houses.

RUTHLESS HARALD AND THE GREAT ESCAPE

One of Harald's Byzantine employers was the Empress Zoe. She was as ruthless as Harald in her own way: she had her husband murdered in his bath, and her second husband became the new emperor. Perhaps distrusting Harald, Zoe accused him of stealing from the royal treasury and had him thrown in prison. Harald escaped and joined a revolution against the empress and her new husband. He caught the new emperor and gouged out his eyes.

By this time Constantinople was getting too dangerous, even for Harald Hardrada. He escaped by boat with a picked group of followers. But out in the narrow waters of the Bosphorus he found that his way was barred by chains slung across the water from bank to bank to stop him. Nothing daunted, Harald slipped his ship over the chains by ordering everyone first to the back of the boat so that it tipped up at the front, then making them all move to the front of the boat when it was halfway over the chain.

HARALD AND THE COATLESS ARMY

Safely back in Scandinavia, Harald became King of Norway. This was where he earned his nickname Hardrada, meaning hard ruler. But Norway wasn't enough for him. His greedy eye soon turned towards England. In 1066 he attacked England with a fleet of three hundred ships and an army of nine thousand men.

But Harald's luck had run out at last. It was September when he invaded England and the weather was still warm. His Vikings took off their leather coats and were marching unprotected when they were surprised by an English army at Stamford Bridge in Yorkshire. Despite the surprise, the Vikings fought bravely and for a while the English were held off by a huge Viking who held the bridge and killed forty men with his axe. Once this giant had been speared from below (by an Englishman in a paddle boat), the end was near. Harald was killed by an arrow in his throat and the Viking army was crushed. With Harald Hardrada's death, the Viking Age in England was finally over.

Or was it?...

WILLIAM TAKES OVER

In 1066, while Harald Hardrada's army invaded England from the north, England was also threatened by Normans from the south.

The Normans were Vikings who had settled in France more than a hundred years earlier after the French king, Charles the Simple, signed a treaty with a Viking called Rollo. In return for promising to obey the French king and for converting to Christianity, Rollo was made lord of most of the lands of what is now Normandy - the land of the Norsemen. The Vikings liked France so much that within a hundred years they had all turned into French-speaking 'Normans', marrying French people and also, no doubt, enjoying a glass of wine for breakfast.

IS MY CROISSANT READY?

In 1066 William, Duke of Normandy, who claimed to be the rightful heir to the throne of England, backed his claim with a massive invasion force, landing on the south coast.

The English army marched south from Stamford Bridge as fast as they could to meet the Normans, but by the time they reached the south coast they were exhausted. At the Battle of Hastings Harold Godwin, the English leader, was killed by an arrow in his eye and William, Duke of Normandy, descendant of the Vikings, won the battle and became William the Conqueror, first Norman king of England.

The Viking conquest of England was finally complete.

DRUNK FOR EVER!
- WELL NOT QUITE

GHASTLY GROVES FOR GLOOMY GODS

The Vikings were the last pagans in western Europe. Their religion was a horrible gloomy religion and offered absolutely no hope and comfort to believers. You had to be pretty brave to believe in it at all and many Vikings didn't.

> We know about pagan Viking religion from poems. In particular a collection of thirty-nine poems called the *Elder Edda*, first written down in 1225 in Iceland but actually much older.

Viking religion involved a lot of sacrifice, including human sacrifice. Sacrifices were made in sacred woods and groves of trees. At their great 'temple' at Uppsala in Sweden there was a festival every nine years where they sacrificed 'nine heads of every living thing that is male' over a period of nine days. The bodies were hung up in the grove. Human sacrifices might be:

- hurled from cliffs

Drowned in wells or bogs

GLUG

Hung

Let's find out what drove them to it ...

THE BEASTLY BEGINNING OF EVERYTHING

Vikings believed that the first living creature was a horrible giant called Ymir who lived on milk from a god-like cow called Authumbla. Ymir was killed by his grandsons, Odin and two brothers. They used his body to make the world:

- PLANTS FROM THE HAIR
- SKY FROM THE SKULL
- MOUNTAINS FROM THE BONES
- CLOUDS FROM THE BRAINS
- SOIL FROM THE FLESH
- OCEANS AND LAKES FROM THE BLOOD

107

THE WORLD ACCORDING TO VIKINGS

You may think that the world is a round ball of matter flying round the Sun. Vikings thought differently. They thought that the Earth was a flat disc surrounded by an ocean.

FOUR DWARFS HELD UP THE SKY.

THE LAND OF JOTUNHEIM, THE ABODE OF THE GIANTS, WAS BEYOND THE OCEAN.

THE EARTH WAS A FLAT DISC CIRCLED BY A GREAT OCEAN.

THE NORNS WERE FATES WHO DECIDED WHAT WOULD HAPPEN IN THE LIVES OF ALL CREATURES.

AN EAGLE WAS AT WAR WITH THE SERPENT IN THE ROOTS.
RATATOSK, A SQUIRREL, CAUSED TROUBLE BETWEEN THE EAGLE AND THE SERPENT.
YGGDRASIL, THE WORLD TREE, HELD UP THE UNIVERSE. IT'S TRUNK WAS ROTTEN.
ASGARD, THE CITADEL OF THE GODS, PERCHED ON A CLIFF.
BIFROST, THE RAINBOW BRIDGE, CONNECTED ASGARD TO EARTH.
MIDGARD, THE LAND OF HUMANS, WAS CIRCLED BY A HIGH FENCE.
NIDHOGG, THE SERPENT, GNAWED AT THE ROOTS OF YGGDRASIL, THE WORLDTREE.
THE WELL OF FATE

ODIN AND LIFE IN ASGARD

Odin was the favourite god of Viking warriors. The bravest slain in battle could expect to end up in his great hall, called Valholl, the hall of the slain - normally called *Valhalla* in English. It had six hundred and forty doorways and the rafters in its roof were spear shafts. There the dead warriors could feast all night and fight all day - until night came again and their wounds were magically healed so that they were ready for another bout of feasting.

Odin's maid-servants were called the *Valkyries* or Choosers of the Slain. In early stories they visited battlefields and ate the corpses of the dead; in later versions they carried fallen warriors off to Valhalla.

Odin himself was no saint. He often travelled in disguise with a grey beard, an old blue cloak and a wide-brimmed hat, riding, on his eight-legged horse, Sleipnir. Wherever he went he caused trouble, hoping to start new fights so that more warriors would be killed. He had many names:

OH DEAR, ODIN

Odin also sacrificed himself to himself by hanging on the Windswept Tree (probably Yggdrasil) seeking the wisdom of the dead.

Viking religion is perhaps the only one where everything gets destroyed in the end and the forces of evil triumph. Only people as tough as the Vikings could bear to believe in it. The end of the world according to the Vikings was called *Ragnarok*, meaning the Doom of the Gods.

THE HORRIBLE END OF EVERYTHING

The gods knew what was going to happen to them, even while they feasted in their palaces in Asgard. They knew that *Midgardsorm*, the World Serpent, lurked deep beneath the ocean and *Fenrir*, an evil wolf, lay bound in a cavern far away.

I'M LOOKING FORWARD TO THE END OF THE WORLD!

The gods knew that as the end drew near, things would start to go wrong for them. Odin's son, Baldur, would be killed by the treachery of an evil half-god called Loki, and from then on nothing would be able to stop the horrible fate which awaited them. The world would be frozen in a terrible winter called the *Fimbul Winter*. There would be earthquakes, the sun would go out, the dwarfs would cower in their rock-dwellings and the chains which bound the forces of evil would be smashed apart - and that would be just the beginning.

Next all Hel would break lose - literally. Fenrir the Wolf would break free from his chains and charge towards Asgard with jaws which stretched from heaven to earth. Midgardsorm the Serpent would lash in anger and the sea would flood over the land. The dead would cross the ocean from Hel, the underworld, in a boat made of dead men's nails.

Finally the giants would ride towards Asgard from the south and all the monsters of land and sea would join their army. *Bifrost*, the Rainbow Bridge, would break under their weight.

Summoned by the horn of Heimdall, the watchman, the gods would take up their weapons and prepare for battle. Odin would lead his band of fallen warriors against Fenrir the Wolf but would be eaten up, although his son would tear Fenrir's jaws apart in vengeance. The god Frey would be killed by the leader of the giants. Heimdall and Loki would kill each other. Thor would kill the serpent but would fall down dead from its poison.

In this battle to end all battles all the gods would be killed, the earth would burst into flame, then in a final horrific catastrophe the earth would sink hissing and sputtering into the sea and steam would cover the stars. It would be the end of everything.

Small wonder that the Vikings took to Christianity. At least it has a happy ending.

SIX FEET UNDER

Vikings seem to have been confused about what happened to them after they were dead - those that weren't chosen to go to Valhalla. On the one hand they thought that they would go to Hel, the underworld; on the other hand they might live on in the grave itself. Sometimes Hel-shoes were tied to a corpse's feet for the long walk to the underworld.

Hel was a misty cold place ruled over by a goddess,

also called Hel. She was not an attractive person: her rotting body was half black and half flesh-coloured. Her palace was called Sleetcold and her dinner plate was called Hunger.

Vikings might be buried with a horse or a boat to help them on the journey. Their graves were usually shaped like ships. The most spectacular of all Viking methods of dealing with the dead was to place the body on a ship and then burn it. This custom is still remembered in the festival of *Up Helly Aa* on the Orkneys, when a specially-built Viking longship is set on fire.

THE TALE OF ASMUND AND THE IRKSOME SLAVE

Whether they went to Hel or stayed on in the grave, it was good for the dead to be buried with some of their possessions so as to make their next life more comfortable. Sometimes a slave or favourite wife was popped into the grave to keep them company. One of the first settlers on Iceland, a man called Asmund, was buried with a boat and a slave. Some time later a passer-by heard Asmund's voice chanting from the grave, saying that he didn't care for the slave's company and would rather be on his own. The grave was opened and the slave removed, and from then on Asmund was silent.

› CLOUD OF GLOOM ‹

WHAT DO YOU BELIEVE IN?

Check it out - are you bad Viking material? (part 5)

1 WHICH OF THESE IS RIGHT?
a The sky is held up by a large pink elephant called Linda.
b The sky is made of a ragged blue cloak.
c The sky is held up by four dwarfs.

2 WHICH OF THESE IS RIGHT?
a Giants help gods fight the forces of destruction.
b Giants are large and friendly but a bit stupid.
c Giants are evil.

Answers on page 122.

WHAT HAPPENED NEXT?

TURN CHRISTIAN - OR ELSE!

QUESTION:
What happens to Vikings if they turn into Christians?

ANSWER:
They stop being Vikings - eventually.

The first wild raiders of Lindisfarne Island in 793 thought Christians were softies who couldn't defend themselves. However, later Vikings saw that there was more to Christianity than an easy source of loot and slaves. They learned that Christianity was the fashionable religion of civilised Europe and that Christians thought that Vikings were a bunch of ignorant barbarians.

One by one Viking kings converted to Christianity. Some kings and leaders were paid to convert, some did it as part of a peace treaty with a Christian king, one or two even believed in it and some of them no doubt just couldn't bear to think about Ragnarok, the Doom of the Gods, any more.

WHAT'S THE MATTER?

I'M SO DEPRESSED.

As for ordinary Vikings, they mostly became Christian because they were told to by their kings. In Scandinavia, the man who started the process was Harald Bluetooth King of Denmark (died 986). Poppa, the missionary who converted him, is said to have proved the power of Christ by putting his hand in a white-hot iron glove. When Harald saw that Poppa's hand was not damaged he converted to Christianity.

The conversion process was continued in Norway, Iceland and Greenland by Olaf Trygvasson, the raider who had smashed the Saxons at the battle of Maldon in 991. Olaf was a tough Viking and he used tough Viking methods to turn people to Christianity, but he was a real softy compared to Olaf the Stout, later Saint Olaf, who finished the conversion of Norway. Saint Olaf maimed, blinded or executed all his subjects who refused to convert.

I CONVERT! I CONVERT!

WHAT A SAINT THAT MAN IS!

Being Christian took the fire out of the Vikings eventually. Pagan habits such as human sacrifice and raiding gradually died out. The Swedes were the last to convert, probably because their big pagan temple at Uppsala was tended by pagan priests. The priests resisted change so as to keep their jobs.

OUR LAST HUMAN SACRIFICE!

THERE, THERE

LAST GASPS

The Viking Age died slowly. Their style of life lingered on in Scandinavia and the Scottish islands, and above all in Iceland, for a long time after it had died out in the rest of Britain and Europe. But the days of the

Vikings were numbered. They were too bold, too bad and too ready to learn new ways to stay Vikings.

The most far-flung Viking outpost of all never had a chance. Greenland was taken over by medieval Norway in 1261. Then as the climate grew colder, Inuit, or Eskimos, moved south and there were violent battles. Contact with Europe gradually died out. All the Viking settlers were dead by 1500. When a ship reached Greenland in 1540, the sailors found only deserted farms.

As for their amazing discovery of America, descendants of the Greenland Vikings were still sailing to Vinland for timber as late as 1347, but eventually the contact was lost - and the memory with it.

Evidence from graves shows that the last Greenlanders were 10 cm shorter on average due to bad diet caused by lack of sunshine to grow vegetables.

YEARS OF FEAR

A Handful of Dates

Random Raids

793	Lindisfarne monastery attacked.
795	First Viking attacks on Ireland and Scotland.
799	Emperor Charlemagne organises defence against Viking raids on Europe.
814	Charlemagne dies. Europe is divided.
825	Vikings settle in the Faroe Islands.

They Came to Stay

839	Vikings spend winter in Ireland for the first time.
841	Dublin founded as Viking base.
844	First Viking attack on Spain.
850	Vikings pass the winter in England for the first time.
859-62	Bjorn Ironsides and Hastein raid Mediterranean.
860	First Rus attack on Constantinople.
865	'Great Heathen Army' invades England.
867	Danes capture York.
870-973	Vikings settle in Iceland.

Britain Bites Back

871-99	Alfred is King of England.
878	Danelaw established, Treaty of Wedmore.

885-86	Siege of Paris.
911	Rollo becomes first Duke of Normandy.
954	End of Viking Kingdom of York, Erik Bloodaxe killed.

Disaster Strikes Again

980	Vikings start raiding England again. Varangian guard started in Constantinople.
986	Start of settlement of Greenland.
1016-35	Canute is King of England.
1042	Danish rule in England ends.
1043	Rus attack Constantinople for the last time.

The End

1066	Harald Hardrada killed at Stamford Bridge. William the Conqueror wins Battle of Hastings.
1347	Greenlanders still sailing to Vinland.
1380	Inuit, or Eskimos, occupy last Viking settlements on Greenland.

Are You Bad Viking Material - Answers.

Score 10 points for each right answer.

Part 1.	Part 2.	Part 3.	Part 4.	Part 5.
1. b	1. b	a or b.	1. c	1. c
2. c	2. b		2. a	2. c
3. b	3. c			

Less than 40   Hopeless - you probably faint at the sight of blood.

40+   Promising - for a wimp.

70+   Excellent - go out and buy an axe.

VILLAINOUS VIKINGS HALL OF FAME

🌀 EGIL SKALLAGRIMSSON

The greatest of all the Viking poets and a great warrior, Egil made his first killing at the age of seven when he struck an eleven-year-old playmate. He was ugly (his nickname means 'bald'), dark, strong and sullen. He saved himself from death at the hands of *Erik Bloodaxe* by composing a poem in Erik's honour in Erik's hall at York.

🌀 ERIK BLOODAXE

A ferocious Viking warrior, the son of *Harald Fairhair*, Erik was King of Norway for a short time from 930, and twice King of York between 948 and 954. He died in an ambush at Stainmore in England in 954.

🌿 Harald Bluetooth

King Harald built the large fortresses in Denmark and converted the country to Christianity. He was fatally wounded in a battle with his own son in 987 and fled the country, dying a few days later.

🌿 Harald Fairhair

Harald's father drowned when he was ten and Harald fought his way to the top, founding the Kingdom of Norway shortly before 900. He had up to twenty sons including *Erik Bloodaxe* and Hakon the Good. He was succeeded by Erik Bloodaxe.

🌿 Harald Hardrada

Perhaps the fiercest Viking of all, Harald fought his first battle in 1030 at the tender age of fifteen, fighting for his relative, King *Olaf the Stout* of Norway. The leader of the opposing army was Svein Forkbeard, son of Canute. Olaf died during the battle and Harald was wounded.

🌿 Hastein

Hastein was known as a master of tricks and was a fearsome freelance raider. The raid round the Mediterranean in 859-62 with Bjorn Ironsides was his most famous adventure. He also led a raid of eighty ships up the Thames in 891.

🌿 Olaf Trygvasson

Olaf was enslaved by pirates when only a child. Spotted by a fellow Swede, he was ransomed and taken to Novgorod where he recognised one of the slavers and killed him with a handaxe. A grandson of

Harald Fairhair, he became King of Norway in 995, converting to Christianity around the same time. He then terrorised his kingdom into converting as well. Died at the Battle of Svold in 1000.

🐾 OLAF THE STOUT

Ruled Norway 1016-28, when he was forced to leave the country following his brutal treatment of Norwegian pagans. He returned to Norway with an army of two thousand warriors in 1030 but was slashed to death with spear, sword and axe at the battle of Stiklarstadir, where his young relative, *Harald Hardrada*, was wounded. After his death Olaf the Stout became Saint Olaf.

🐾 ROLLO

Before he was made Duke of Normandy in 911 Rollo had been raiding in France for several years. In 912 he converted to Christianity and settled down to rule his new dukedom. Rollo may have been the same person as a Viking called *Hrolf the Ganger* or *Walker*, so-called because he was so big no horse could carry him.

INDEX

Alfred, King 92 - 95, 97, 121
Arabs 14, 79, 80, 85, 86
Anglo-Saxon Chronicle 18, 94
Asgard 109, 113
Asser, Bishop 94
Aud the Deep-Minded 34, 37

Baths 28
Battle-Axe People 12
Battles
    Hastings 105, 122
    Maldon 98, 118
    Stainmore 123
    Stamford Bridge 103, 104, 122
    Stiklarstadir 125
    Svold 125
Berserkers 58, 60
Bifrost 109, 113
Birka 80
Bjarni 74, 76, 77
Bjorn Ironsides 89, 121, 124
Blood-Eagle 91
Blood soup 24
Bluetooth, King Harald 118

Canute, King 100, 101, 122, 124
Charlemagne, Emperor 14, 121
Charles the Simple, King 104

Charles the Bald, King 53
Columbus 74
Constantinople 79, 86, 87, 88, 101, 102, 121, 122
Crafts and craftsmen 81 - 83
    Gripping Beast style 82

Danegeld 53, 98
Danelaw 91, 95, 121
Danevirke 60
Divorce 31
Duels 40, 41, 57
Dwarfs 108, 112

Egil Skallagrimsson 1, 47, 123
Elder Edda 106
Ella, King 91
Erik Bloodaxe 97, 122, 123, 124
Erik the Red 73, 74, 77
Eskimos - see Inuit
Ethelred the Unready 99

Fenrir 112 - 114
Floki 71
Feasts 38, 46, 47, 49
Freydis 33, 34, 77
Futhark 50

Gadar 70
Games 49

Giants 108, 113
Gods
  Baldur 112
  Frey 114
  Freyya 17, 19
  Loki 112, 114
  Heimdall 113, 114
  Odin (or Woden) 16, 17, 58, 91, 107, 110 - 112, 113
  Thor 17, 70, 114
  Tyr (or Tiw) 16
Galleys 62
Godwin, Harold 105
Great Heathen Army 91, 121
Gunnbjorn 73
Guthrith 34
Guthrum 95

Hakon the Good, King 124
Harald Hardrada 101 - 104, 122, 124, 125
Harald Bluetooth, King 118, 124
Harald Fairhair, King 123, 124, 125
Hastein 89, 121, 124
Hedeby 80, 81
Hel 113 - 115
Hrolf the Ganger - see Rollo
Hjortspring Ship 62
Human sacrifice 106, 119
Huns 14, 15

Inuit 74, 120, 122

Jotunheim 108

Kamban, Grim 69, 70
Knorrs 64, 65

L'Anse-aux-Meadows 78
Landnamabok 72
Leif Eriksson 33, 74, 76
Lindisfarne 6, 7 - 9, 15, 52, 117, 121
Longhouses 22, 23
Longships 61, 62 - 67

Marriage 31
Midgard 109
Midgardsorm 112, 113

Nadod 71
Normans 104,
Norns 108, 109

Olaf the Stout, King 119, 124, 125
Olaf Trygvasson 57, 62, 98, 118, 124

Papars 70, 72
Pattern-welding 55
Poetry 48
Poppa 118
Punishments 43, 44
Pytheas 12

Ragnar 90, 91

Ragnarok 112, 118
Ratatosk 109
Ribe 80
Rollo 104, 122, 125
Runes 18, 50
Rus 14, 84 - 88, 121, 122

Sagas
　Erik's Saga 78
　General 18, 33. 47, 48, 50, 58
　Greenlanders' Saga 78
Saxons 18, 90, 93, 95, 96, 118
Sea battles 63
Shieldwall 57
Sleipnir 111
Snorri Thorfinnsson 34
Snorri Sturluson 48
Svein Forkbeard 99, 100, 124

Things 26, 41, 42, 45
Thorfinn Karlsefni 34
Thorhall the Hunter 76

Up Helly Aa 115
Uppsala 106, 119

Valhalla 110, 114
Valkyries 110
Varangian Guard 88, 101, 122
Viking, meaning of word 13
Vinland 75, 76
Volvas 34

Wedmore, Treaty of 121
William the Conqueror 104, 105, 122
Women 11, 27, 29 - 34, 46

Yggdrasil 109, 111

Zoe, Empress 102

About the Author

Bob Fowke is a well-known author of children's information books. Writing under various pen names and with various friends and colleagues, he has created around fifty unusual and entertaining works on all manner of subjects.

There's always more to Fowke books than meets the eye - so don't be misled by the humorous style (just check out the index at the end of this book!). They're just the thing if you want your brain to bulge and your information banks to burble.

Bob Fowke is the youngest son of a Sussex vicar, and spent his childhood in the large, draughty vicarage of the village of Fletching (where the famous historian Edward Gibbon is buried). After years of travel and adventure, he now lives quietly in Shropshire.

What They Don't Tell You About...
ORDER FORM

0 340 71330 5	ART	£3.99
0 340 63622 X	QUEEN VICTORIA	£3.99
0 340 69349 5	LIVING THINGS	£3.99
0 340 67093 2	SHAKESPEARE	£3.99
0 340 69350 9	STORY OF SCIENCE	£3.99
0 340 65614 X	ANCIENT EGYPTIANS	£3.99
0 340 68612 X	WORLD WAR II	£3.99
0 340 71329 1	PLANET EARTH	£3.99
0 340 71328 3	ANCIENT GREEKS	£3.99
0 340 68995 1	STORY OF MUSIC	£3.99
0 340 73611 9	OLYMPICS	£3.99
0 340 78805 4	WORLD WAR I	£3.99
0 340 78806 2	CHARLES I AND THE CIVIL WAR	£3.99
0 340 78807 0	THE COLD WAR	£3.99
0 340 78808 9	TUDORS	£5.99

All Hodder Children's books are available at your local bookshop or newsagent, or can be ordered direct from the publisher. Just write to the address below. Prices and availability subject to change without notice.

Hodder Children's Books, Cash Sales Department, Bookpoint, 130 Milton Park, Abingdon, Oxon, OX14 4SB, UK.
Email address: orders@bookpoint.co.uk

Please enclose a cheque or postal order made payable to Bookpoint Ltd to the value of the cover price and allow the following for postage and packing:
UK & BFPO - £1.00 for the first book, 50p for the second book, and 30p for each additional book ordered, up to a maximum charge of £3.00.
OVERSEAS & EIRE - £2.00 for the first book, £1.00 for the second book, and 50p for each additional book.

If you have a credit card you may order by telephone - (01235) 400414 (lines open 9 am - 6 pm, Monday to Saturday; 24 hour message answering service). Alternatively you can send a fax on 01235 400454.